S0-AAA-019

# Cheap Dates

# Cheap Dates

## Fun, Creative, and Romantic Dates That Won't Break Your Budget

Steven C. Smith

PRIMA PUBLISHING

3000 Lava Ridge Court • Roseville, California 95661
(800) 632-8676 • www.primalifestyles.com

© 2001 by Steven C. Smith

All rights reserved. No part of this book may be reproduced or transmitted in any form or by any means, electronic or mechanical, including photo-copying, recording, or by any information storage or retrieval system, without written permission from Prima Publishing, except for the inclu-sion of brief quotations in a review.

PRIMA PUBLISHING and colophon are trademarks of Prima Communica-tions Inc., registered with the United States Patent and Trademark Office.

All products mentioned in this book are trademarks of their respective companies.

**Library of Congress Cataloging-in-Publication Data**
Smith, Steven (Steven C.)
   Cheap dates : fun, creative, and romantic dates that won't break your budget / Steven Smith.
      p.   cm.
   Includes index.
   ISBN 0-7615-3414-8
   1. Dating (Social customs)  2. Budgets, Personal.  I. Title.
HQ801 .S658 2001
646.7'7—dc21                                                        2001021544
01  02  03  04  HH  10  9  8  7  6  5  4  3  2  1
Printed in the United States of America

## How to Order

Single copies may be ordered from Prima Publishing, 3000 Lava Ridge Court, Roseville, CA 95661; telephone (800) 632-8676. Quantity discounts are also available. On your letterhead, include information concerning the intended use of the books and the number of books you wish to purchase.

**Visit us online at www.primalifestyles.com**

To Mom and Dad,
whose love and support are never ending.

# CONTENTS

# ACKNOWLEDGMENTS

Thanks to my older brother and coach Greg Smith, who generously shared with me many creative dating tips when I first became old enough to date, and who helped make my first date a memorable one by trusting me to take out his brand new convertible! To my brother Bob Smith, who continues to be a major source of inspiration in my life and in my business. To my sister Cherie Jenkins, for her encouragement and enthusiasm. And, of course, to my father and mother Harold and Patricia Smith, for their continual flow of love, support, and prayers over the years and for giving us kids the awesome gift of witnessing their recent 50th wedding anniversary.

To my nephews and nieces, who make me proud to be their uncle and for whom many of the dates in this book I was inspired to write: Reggie and Casey Parks; Kerry, Riley, Andy, Sari Jane, and Jordan Jenkins; Tyson, Tregg, and Hannah Smith; Aaron, Angela, and Allison Smith; and Peyton, Chris, and Juanita Parks.

Additional thanks to my friends and relatives for their contributions, valuable feedback, and willingness to participate in many of the dates in this book: Rick and Andrea Caudillo, Rosalyn Kay, Terry Higgins, Donna Ramos, Brad Wiens, JoAnne Bocchi Kenney, Todd "Tiny" Thomas, Michael and Angela McClure, Jim Friesen, Rhonda Henry, Steve Moeller, David Lewis, Brian Bowman, David Dickerson, Mitch Willett, Andrew Fouch, Cynthia Sliwa, Joe Snead, Jeff Finger, CJ Burns, Mike Hyder, and Vicki Mauricio.

I am especially grateful to the following individuals who helped to make this book a reality: Harold Reynolds, for your valuable friendship and for pointing me in the right direction; Melissa Helms, for your generous support and guidance; Marc Moore, for seeing something special in the making; and to my editor Dawn Josephson, Cameo Publications, for your expert advice, editing, and direction.

A special thanks to Carolina Portillo Franco, Tom Kunke, Joe Valentino, and Sue Ward for inspiring me to "press on" and stay the course and for believing I had something special to offer. To Vic Madden, Steve Lyons, and Ron Hunt, for always asking me the question, "When is your dating book getting published?"—you were a major source of motivation.

Thanks to Denise Sternad, Tara Mead, Pat Henshaw, Monica Thomas, Brenda Ginty, and the other amazing staff at Prima Publishing, for making this such an enjoyable and memorable experience and who were helpful and accommodating every step of the way.

Finally, I'd like to acknowledge the many individuals and couples of all ages, who over the years were willing to share their time, insights, and personal experiences, which all helped to shape the outcome of this book.

# INTRODUCTION

**D**ating. We love it. We hate it. No matter what our feelings about it, at some time in our lives we all must go through it. Dating can be difficult, and it can be a particular challenge to come up with a terrific date idea that is also affordable. *Cheap Dates: Fun, Creative, and Romantic Dates That Won't Break Your Budget* is designed to help you become a more confident dater, to eliminate the stress that dating sometimes causes, and to encourage you to get out of the usual dinner-and-a-movie rut. It is filled with hundreds of creative and timeless date ideas, each of which costs less than $50. The dates range from the wildly outrageous to the more subdued, so there's bound to be some perfect date ideas for you.

No matter what stage of life you're currently in—whether you're a teen just beginning to date, a single adult in pursuit of meaningful dating relationships, or a married couple committed to the long haul—you're never too young or too old for creative dating.

This insightful and humorous book will become your number one reference guide for memorable dates, and it will be a lifesaver for anyone who wants to rekindle an old flame or ignite a new romance. The various categories make it an easy-to-use quick reference guide for last-minute planning.

And because not every date is destined to be a discount date, this book also offers "Splurge Dates," an entire chapter dedicated to those times when it's appropriate to spend your money. As a bonus, throughout this book you will find tips to help spice up your date: charming ideas that you can incorporate into any date to make it memorable. After all, the thoughtful things you say or do on a date often stand out the most: the rose you spontaneously purchase for your date or your spur-of-the-moment moonlight serenade.

At the back of the book, you'll find a collection of dating coupons for you to have fun with. Ideas for the coupons run the gamut from a video night to a weekend getaway.

Use this book for your next dating adventure. Keep it in your backpack, in the glove compartment of your car, or anywhere within reach. One quick glance, and you'll be on your way to bringing excitement and vitality to your dating relationships without having to invest extensive time or money.

# How I Came to Write This Book

I first had the idea for this book when I was in college at Oregon State University. I was a dedicated student-athlete and spent most of my time either on the baseball field, in the library, or in the classroom. There seemed to be very little time for dating. Coming up with a good date plan was difficult, and having to get by on a student budget didn't help.

It wasn't until I attended a discussion on dating relationships at a campus life fellowship meeting that I learned the importance of the "friends first" approach to dating—an important step that is often left out of today's relationships. That evening I walked away with the understanding that a great way to make sure you get to know your dating partner is to spend quality time together doing creative activities that promote communication, fun, and laughter.

I adopted this concept in my next dating relationship and created many fond memories, all the while participating in numerous zany and delightful activities with a special person. We had so much fun together that our friends began to take notice. Soon the creative dating bug began to rub off on them as well. In no time at all, we were all coming up with creative ideas for dates that were easy, fun, and always something to anticipate.

After college, I spent several years as a minor league professional baseball player. During my travels, I spent much of my free time interviewing people, both young and old, about their most memorable and creative dating experiences. I was surprised by how many people struggled to come up with just one creative date idea to share. Immediately, I saw the need for a dating-idea book designed to help couples avoid the snare of routine and repetitive dating. This book was written to fulfill that need.

Over the years, I have enjoyed assisting others with planning creative ideas for dates and other special occasions. I recall a friend who consulted with me on several occasions for date ideas to share with someone in whom he was interested. For the first month, I would receive one or two calls per week from him. It wasn't long before he began to come up with many great ideas on his own. The calls for advice began to taper off. I didn't hear from him for about six months, until one day he called to ask for my opinion on a creative idea for the date on which he planned to propose marriage. Today he and his wife are happily married and still dating in Oregon.

# How to Use This Book

If you're in search of that ideal creative date but are completely lost for an idea, don't panic. Let the Creative Dating Key serve as your dating compass. With the Creative Dating Key as your date-planning companion, you'll never be at a loss for the perfect date idea.

Each date is preceded by one of the following Creative Dating icons. Pick an icon that best fits your dating goal and look for dates bearing that icon. In a matter of seconds, this key will help you navigate through the multitude of date ideas and pinpoint the ideal date for your occasion.

# Creative Dating Key

 **Friends First Date**
*No commitment, just pals*

 **Great First Date**
*For the perfect first impression*

 **Relationship-Building Date**
*More than just friends*

 **Sizzle Date**
*Romantically charged!*

 **Last-Minute Date**
*Something quick, something easy*

 **Out-of-the-Doghouse Date**
*When it's time to come crawling back*

 **Married Couples Date**
*Keep the spark going*

 **Anything Goes Date**
*Whatever and wherever you want it to be*

# Now It's Your Turn

Armed with your dating guidebook, you're now on your way to creating memorable, enjoyable, and affordable dates of your own. So find that someone special, get those creative juices flowing, and prepare yourself for an incredible time. Who would have thought that dating could be so much fun, so cheap, and so very, very creative?

It is my hope that you will benefit richly from the ideas in this book, just as many others have, and that you will learn the art of going on a cheap date without feeling like a cheapskate. Happy dating!

# An Obligatory Disclaimer

*Warning:* This book is intended for entertainment purposes only. Although most of the creative date ideas have been field-tested by real daters, the author and publisher make no claims as to any date's likely success or final outcome. If you're unsure of a date's legality in your geographic location, check with your local police department or city hall.

When choosing a date, keep local conditions in mind. The Island Divider Date, on page 115, for example, works nicely in a place like Des Moines, Iowa, where some of the median islands are planted with flowering trees and look like miniature gardens. This date would be a little risky and noisy, and probably not all that pleasant, in a place like Los Angeles!

Exercise caution when undertaking athletic or thrill-seeking dates, such as the Rooftop Rendezvous or Ice-Blocking. Also, keep in mind that these dates are for all ages. Some are geared toward the kid in you, while others are for a more mature outing. As ever, dating is done at your own risk!

# Cheap Dates

# CHAPTER 1

# FUN AND FRUGAL DATES

D ating can certainly take its toll on our bank accounts. With today's rising costs, frequent trips to the ATM can become a requirement for even a modest night out on the town. Whether you're a discount dater by nature or by necessity, you can plan a cheap date without feeling like a cheapskate.

While many people believe that dating on a budget is a bore, nothing could be further from the truth. In fact, even if you do not have to keep a close watch on your finances, there are many fun and affordable dates waiting to be experienced, such as the Dollar-Night-Out Date or the Due-for-Something-New Date. So whether you're a starving college student trying to impress your date on meager funds or a well-to-do married couple looking for some new and exciting date ideas that won't drain the family inheritance, this chapter will give you many creative examples of how to have a quality date without breaking the bank.

 ## Historical Tour Date

Did you know that Gilroy, California, boasts of being the garlic capital of the world? (Not even a giant breath mint could freshen up this town!) Or that the town of Dallas, Oregon, once had the dubious distinction of being the world's leading producer of prunes? (Nothing but "regular" folk living there!)

So how about your town—what's it famous for? Make a date to find out. Spend part of your day together browsing through the historical records at the library, and then tour locations and well-known landmarks. Have a picnic on the site where the pioneers settled and made claim to what resides today as your hometown.

## Share-a-Crab Date

Head down to the local fish market or ocean diner and pick up a couple of whole cooked crabs. Take them to a fun location, such as a pier, a boat dock, or a wind-protected cove at the beach, and enjoy a mouthwatering lunch with your date.

# ★Spice It Up!

### Note in the Popcorn Tub

If you're like most movie-going couples, there's no doubt you'll be sharing a tub of hot popcorn at the theater. Once the popcorn tub is almost half empty, secretly drop in a note while your date's attention is focused on the movie screen. Then wait in anticipation until your date reaches in for another handful of popcorn, only to clutch the special note. Be sure to bring a keychain light to illuminate the message, which might read something like, "Love is . . . sharing a tub of popcorn at the movies," or "Love is . . . wiping my hands on your jeans after eating a handful of popcorn," or "Don't be afraid to hold my hand."

Bring all of the essential tools required to crack the crustaceans: shell cracker, baby crab forks, cleaning wipes, and paper plates. Most important, don't forget your fisherman's hats to protect yourselves from the curious seagulls flying overhead, who just might drop in for an unwelcomed visit.

To make this date an entire day's event, rent a few crab rings and catch your own crabs off the dock. Bring them home and cook them in a kettle for a crab feast fit for a king.

If you don't live near a seaport or an ocean city, go to the seafood section of your local grocery store to buy your crabs. Cook them at home, then enjoy them at a creative sandy location (a sand volleyball court at a city park, a golf course sand trap, or even your neighbor's sandbox!). Turn it into the next best thing to being at the beach.

 **Grandparents Date**

A visit to your grandparents' house traditionally means a holiday family gathering and a nap on the couch after a belly-busting home-cooked meal. But with this date, your grandparents are the main attraction and participants in a thoughtful and creative date.

Take some time out from your busy schedules and do something special with your grandparents. You and your date can help Grandpa out with some of the outside chores, like mowing the lawn or chopping some wood. Then assist Grandma around the house with the laundry and kitchen duties, or help her pick a bouquet of flowers during a walk through the flower garden. After a full afternoon of chores, retire to the front porch and enjoy some of Grandma's homemade peach cobbler and ice cream as you relax and listen to them take turns sharing some of their fondest memories as a dating couple.

## Dutch Treat Date

Pitch in a few dollars each and try to come up with the most creative date imaginable with the money you have pooled together. Attempt to stretch your funds as far as they can go. Buy a newspaper and solve the word puzzle at a creative location; purchase a disposable camera and take pictures of each other being silly; share a malt at the corner drugstore and play old songs on the jukebox. Combine your funds and your ideas to make this date truly unforgettable.

To be certain you find a date who is comfortable with paying half, consider going on a date with your ex! Before you do, however, be sure to carefully measure this date's potential for disaster, or you might get stuck with the bill and a solo taxi ride home.

## Monster Cookie Date

Go to a local cookie shop and team up with your date to devour a monster cookie together. Be sure to lug along a carton of milk to share, as it will make your "meal" complete.

If the shop doesn't carry a cookie big enough to satisfy your ferocious appetites, ask them if they'll do a special order of monumental proportion, or consider making your own. Mix up a batch of your favorite cookie dough and bake a creation big enough to satisfy you both. Buy some frosting and have a cookie-decorating contest. Be sure to make extras to share with your friends and neighbors.

## Dollar-Night-Out Date

Plan an entire evening where you spend no more than $1 (or as close to $1 as possible) for each activity. Select a venue for this date that will work well with the one-buck budget plan, such as a novelty gift shop, a swap meet, or a college campus.

Here are a few ideas for you and your date to consider. Do one, do two, or do them all. Let your budget be your guide.

* Rent a dollar movie (or check one out for free at the library).
* Take your pictures together in a photo booth.
* Snack on a dollar's worth of your favorite penny candy.
* Go to the arcade and spend four quarters on video games.
* For dinner, buy some pizza by the slice.
* Share a scoop of ice cream for dessert.
* Buy a small cup of coffee and a newspaper and read the funnies to each other.

## Coffeehouse Date

Let's face it, coffee shops are in. You can hardly walk a city block without tripping over the coffee beans spilling out onto the streets. As unique as they are from one another, one thing is certain: Each provides a selection of caffeinated beverages sure to provide the pep for an entire evening of conversation and fun.

Pick a beanery that best suits your preferences in coffee and atmosphere, and spend an evening enjoying the tastes and aromas of assorted coffees brewed to perfection. Order a couple of cappuccinos, and then cozy up to a table for two as you listen to an acoustic guitarist play some soothing sounds.

Pass the time with a game of backgammon or chess, read a book to each other, or simply spend the evening visiting and people-watching while sharing a mouthwatering dessert. This is a great after-dinner activity.

 **Report Card Date**

Anyone who's been in school knows what a challenge it can be to balance school with dating. It can be difficult to concentrate on your homework when you can't keep your eyes off your cute study partner. But here's an idea to scribble in your notes that is sure to bridge the study versus dating gulf.

Plan an "end-of-the-semester" dinner date with your study partner. Together, plan a Report Card Date Menu in which the meal that each of you eat will depend on the letter grade you each receive. For example, if your final grade is an A, then you will enjoy a steak dinner; a B will earn you a pizza; and so on. The higher the grade you receive in your class, the higher the quality of your meal.

Here's an example:

**Report Card Date Menu**

**A** Steak dinner

**B** Pizza

**C** Hot dog

**D** Peanut butter and jelly sandwich

**F** Bread and water

Study hard! You don't want to be slurping down a hot dog while your date is savoring filet mignon.

# ★Spice It Up!

## A Textbook Moment for a Message

Here's a special thought to make your next study date one to remember. Once you've made sure the coast is clear, slip a little message into your date's textbook (a page or two beyond the last page read). Once your date has resumed reading, watch with great expectancy as your date turns the page, only to discover the special message you have inserted. Have the note read something like: "Good luck on your finals. I'm pulling for you." What a great way to initiate a study break.

 ## Due-for-Something-New Date

Fitness experts agree that variety is an important factor in avoiding a plateau in your workout regimen. The same is true with dating. Too many routine dinner-and-a-movie outings can put you and your significant other in a dating rut.

To keep your dating life healthy and fit, make a date to try something new—something you've never done before. Be daring and try something out of the ordinary. Take a dance lesson together, sit in on a town hall meeting, race mini–Grand Prix cars, or go to the gym and work out.

Go somewhere you've never gone before, such as a famous historical landmark, another section of town, or a nearby city. If you're content with the dinner-and-a-movie formula, then at least try a new kind of food. Go out for some sushi, Rocky Mountain oysters, or a veggie burger.

## Underdog Date

Life is full of activities and events that are competitive in nature, whether in politics, relationships (heaven forbid), sports, or business. And all of us will, from time to time, catch ourselves rooting for the little man, the mom-and-pop enterprise, the dark horse . . . the underdog! So team up to create a date plan full of ideas and activities that honor the less-favored. Here are some suggestions to get you started:

* ✳ Visit a locally owned bookstore rather than a national chain.
* ✳ Eat at a "dive" or a hole-in-the-wall restaurant instead of a well-established one. (You just might find the food and the service to be beyond honorable mention.)
* ✳ Go to a high school junior varsity football game (usually free) instead of the varsity game, and root for the team with the worst record.
* ✳ Although it may take a bit longer, take a bike taxi (it's more romantic, too!) instead of a regular taxi.
* ✳ Shop at a "clothes for less" store or an outlet mall rather than a department store.
* ✳ Instead of going to an amusement park, go to a city park and take turns giving each other an "underdog" on the swings.

Whatever "underdog" activity you choose, give your full support and encouragement to whatever or whomever is least likely to win.

## Community Performing Arts Date

Attending a community chorale concert is definitely a cheap date and a lot of fun for the price, and you just might hear some wonderful music. Stay for refreshments and chat with the performers; then play critics and write up a review of the concert over cups of coffee.

A similar idea is to see a high school musical production or a recital by the students of a local conservatory or ballet academy. It's cheap, entertaining, and charming. Recitals by students in college music programs also are often free or very inexpensive.

After the show, create a few performing arts of your own—with your lips! On your drive home together, whenever you and your date see an oncoming car with one headlight burned out, shout out the word "perdittle." For each "perdittle," your date is to award you a kiss. See how many "perdittles" you can collect. You'll soon discover that it does pay to keep your eyes on the road!

For the real finale, play Modittle. It's similar to Perdittle, except that you shout "modittle" when you see an oncoming car that is driving at night with no headlights on. Because it is rare to see cars driving at night without their headlights on, a "modittle" is good for two kisses! (That's just a recommendation. Feel free to add "mo" kisses if you like.)

# CHAPTER 2

# ROMANTIC DATES

L ooking to add a little romance to your new dating relationship? Or perhaps you're in a long-term relationship and feel it's time to rekindle the sentimental and amorous moments from the early stages of your courtship. Whatever your current situation, don't despair. It's never too late to be romantic, nor is it ever too late to be romanced. This chapter is full of creative ideas that are sure to add romance to any dating relationship. So get ready to restore the passion that's so vital to keeping the flame burning brightly!

 ## Oceanside Picnic Date

A romantic experience that incorporates the unexpected, the Oceanside Picnic Date is one that is destined for the memory books. As far as your date is concerned, it's an impromptu stroll along the beach shortly before sunset (or a local lake or river if you aren't near the coast). To you, however, it's a preplanned affair that involves fun, food, and some help from friends.

While you're on your way to pick up your date, have a friend go to the beach on your behalf to set up a romantic picnic at a predetermined location: a blanket, a picnic basket full of delicious fare, a tune box playing romantic music, a single rose in a vase, and two wine glasses (but not the bottle of wine—that comes later!).

As you and your date begin your walk down the beach, have your friend, who's been safely guarding your picnic site, leave the scene unnoticed when you come within 50 to 100 yards of the picnic. As your date watches with surprise and delight, sit down, begin to serve up some cheese as an appetizer, and then appear to realize that there's no wine to go with it. With an "I can't believe I forgot the wine" look on your face, draw your date's attention to the ocean surf, only to find someone (another one of your friends) paddling to shore in an ocean kayak to hand-deliver the purposely forgotten bottle of wine. (If you really want to be creative, arrange to have a scuba-diving friend surface from the shallow waves and fin up to shore to uncork and pour your wine before treading back to the breakwater.)

This date is sure to make a big splash no matter what the occasion!

## Motorcycle Ride Date

Motorcycle dates are clutch, in more ways than one. First of all, they provide a great opportunity for intimacy as well as adventure. Second, when you "clutch" down and kick it into gear, your date gets to "clutch" onto you with a grip that'll last for miles!

For this date, pick a destination such as a remote, scenic location that has special meaning to you (or at least it will after this date), or plan to ride to a nearby city and attend a special event together. When you are on a motorcycle, event parking is easy and convenient. Wherever you go, be sure to take country roads so you can increase your chances of seeing some horses grazing along the roadside, which you can pull over to pet. It's good to keep the destination under twenty miles because you won't be able to talk much during the ride.

Taking a picnic lunch with you on the motorcycle would be a big plus. If that's not possible, an outdoor lunch at a quaint roadside cafe would be a great alternative.

This is a great date that appeals to all of the senses:

* Touch: Enjoy the feeling of holding tight to, and being held onto by, your date.
* Sight: Take in the beautiful landscape along a scenic route.
* Taste: Stop along the roadside to pick and eat some wild blackberries.
* Smell: A whiff of the fresh country air will clear your mind and revive your spirit.
* Hearing: There's nothing like the sound of a revving engine in concert with the whipping sounds of the breeze blowing by your ears.

Once you reach your destination, try to find an alternate route home so you can experience different sights and sounds.

 ## Outdoor Home-Dinner Date

Preparing a home-cooked meal for your date, or surprising your spouse with a full-course dinner at the end of a hectic day, can be utterly romantic. The smell of certain foods in the air, the scent of burning candles, a romantic collection of instrumental music playing in the background—all appeal to the romantic senses.

To make this creative dinner date truly special, arrange to have dinner outdoors on your deck during a warm spring or summer evening. (Other locations may include your patio, backyard garden, gazebo, or rooftop garden.) Decorate your table with a centerpiece of flowers, romantic candles, a

# ⋆⋆Spice It Up!

## Say It with Flowers

When was the last time you greeted your date with flowers upon arriving at her door? What a classy way to begin a date. Any girl would be delighted to receive a bouquet of flowers, whether they're freshly picked from the garden or nicely arranged from the floral shop. Flowers can leave a lasting impression because they can be kept for many days following your date, and perhaps for months if your date chooses to dry them.

Ladies, when was the last time you bought flowers for your man? You'd be surprised how special an arrangement of flowers can make a man feel.

---

tablecloth, and dinner settings. Include some bamboo torch lights for illumination. From within your home, bring out plants and furniture items to help create a cozy atmosphere.

As a clincher, woo your date with a surprise musical serenade. As you settle down for dinner, you begin to hear romantic melodies from a violin playing in the distance. Eventually the violinist (who is a friend of yours, or a friend of a friend) meanders up the stairs and serenades the two of you for an hour.

Once the music is over and your dinner finished, conclude the evening with some dessert and a stroll around the yard or block. Your date will be impressed by your thoughtful and romantic touch.

## Just Dessert Date

One of the most romantic images by far is of two people out on a date, sitting across a candlelit table from one another, lost in great conversation at a restaurant known for its romantic charm and ambiance. Although such restaurants are also often known for their fancy prices, that factor poses no barrier for the smart dater on a budget.

The Just Dessert Date describes exactly what you plan to do—have just dessert. By doing this, you can enjoy many of the benefits of being at a trendy restaurant, without breaking your budget. Stretch out your time together by mulling over all of the mouthwatering dessert options. If the desserts are of gargantuan proportion, consider teaming up on one dessert and asking the waiter to bring you two forks or spoons. In most cases, however, you'll want to each choose a dessert and share a bite or two of each other's choice.

A little dessert wine or gourmet coffee may be a nice complement to your Just Dessert Date. In return for the generous dessert portions and coffee refills you'll likely enjoy as you share conversation and laughs with your date, show your appreciation to your waiter with a generous tip.

## Sentimental Flashback Date

Do you remember your very first date with your spouse or sweetheart? Can you recall the nervous anticipation—the butterflies in your stomach, the sweaty palms?

When it comes time for you to celebrate your next special anniversary, consider stepping back in time to relive the advent of your relationship with the Sentimental Flashback Date. Recapture every moment of your first date. Go to the same restaurant, wear the same clothes (or similar outfits), and visit the same fun places. Play songs from that era to elicit warm thoughts and memories from yesteryear. If you took pictures while on your first date, bring along a camera and do your best to reproduce your poses. Your beloved will be newly enamored with you and your thoughtfulness and inspiration.

 ## Message-in-a-Bottle Date

Here's a memory that will be cherished for a lifetime. Invite your special someone to take a romantic stroll along the beach at the ocean or a nearby lake. Stealthily reach into your backpack and remove a vintage bottle that contains a poem you've written on a piece of parchment that you've ruffled, stained, and singed along the edges to give it a look of antiquity. While your date is distracted by some seagulls or other wildlife, drop the bottle at the water's edge. Keeping one eye on your date and one eye on the bottle, wait patiently until your date discovers the bottle that has apparently just washed up on the shore.

Reading the message out loud, your date finds it to be a romantic poem that expresses one person's feelings toward another. As the final passage is read, your date will be astonished to learn just who the author really is. At that moment, tell your date how wonderful you feel about your relationship.

 ## Poetic Date

You don't have to be Robert Frost or Emily Dickinson to do poetic justice to this date. If you can say, "Roses are red, violets are blue," then troubadour or not, this date is for you!

Take your date to a creative location brimming with inspiration (a hill beneath a shady tree overlooking a meadow, a cliff with a spectacular view of the valley below, or even a ledge peering over a building demolition site!). Give each other a few minutes of solitude in which to write a poem to the other. Express your feelings with a romantic verse or a funny limerick.

Once you've completed your poems, read them to one another with sincere devotion or romantic cheer, whichever best fits your disposition. Next, scribe a poem together, taking turns composing one line at a time and melding your thoughts together. Later, have your poem(s) written in calligraphy and mounted in frames so that each of you can have a special keepsake from your Poetic Date.

 **Sunset Date**

One of the most romantic places on Earth is the beach during a sunset. That's why it's one of the most popular locations for dating couples. Here you can spend several hours lolling around in the warm sand as you anticipate the final dip of the sun over the horizon. Pass the time by enjoying all that the beach has to offer: share a picnic near the pier, fly a kite, take a barefoot stroll along the seashore, chase and be chased by the waves, build a sand castle together.

After a time of fun and frolicking, sit down and view one of nature's most spectacular moments—a sunset. Admire the beauty of the glowing orange and red as the sun dips calmly below the horizon. Make a wish upon the first visible evening star that appears in the sky. To make this a signature date, grab a piece of driftwood and use it to etch each other's initials in the sand, enveloped by a large heart shape.

To kindle all of the romance this date has to offer, build a bonfire, if permitted, to keep you both warm and snuggly as you extend your time together. If you live inland, enjoy the sunset just about anywhere: behind the mountains, across a large meadow, or at the end of an airport runway.

 ## Romancing the Snow Date

Regardless of the season, everyone loves to be romanced! If it's wintertime, consider the Romancing the Snow Date. Take a day trip to a ski resort area nestled amid the pristine snow-capped mountains.

Experience the charm of Main Street villages that provide casual, friendly, and down-to-earth hospitality. There's always a lot of "off the slope" action awaiting you. Boutiques, galleries, bistros, coffeehouses, and restaurants are great places to visit.

Lure yourselves outdoors for a time to delight in some snow-filled activities: build a snowman, challenge some kids to a friendly snowball fight, take a gondola ride to the top of the mountain's ski run, enjoy a romantic moonlit sleigh ride, go ice skating, and more!

 ## Fireside Date

Another romantic date worth considering on a cold winter's evening is the Fireside Date. A warm, crackling fire illuminating the living room, a CD carousel filled with hours of romantic background music, a platter of freshly prepared hors d'oeuvres, and a kettle of hot, steamy apple cider are all you need to put this date into action.

# ★★Spice It Up!

## Love Is . . . Comic Strip

Recall from the past all the special things your special someone has done for you, or the great efforts he or she has made that make you feel special and loved, which can often go unnoticed. Communicate them by creating your own "Love is . . ." comic strips. Your personalized comic strip might read something like, "Love is . . . lending me your jacket to keep warm on a chilly evening saunter" or "Love is . . . being given a piggy-back ride across a creek full of crawdads."

Whatever the kind deed, find creative ways to communicate your comic creations. Place them on the refrigerator door with a magnet. Tape them to the person's computer screen. Sneak them into your honey's wallet or coat pocket to be discovered later. For the ultimate effect, get up early and tape them on the first page of the funnies section of the morning newspaper.

Enjoy each other's scintillating conversation. Read a favorite short story to each other. Entertain each other with a friendly game of backgammon or chess. Enjoy laughs as you comb through old school yearbooks and photo albums.

As the evening progresses, put on a pot of coffee and cuddle up on the sofa to watch a classic movie you've rented. Midway through the movie, take an intermission and go for a brief evening saunter around the block before returning for the second half. Place another log on the fire to ensure that the essence of this date keeps burning bright.

## Great Day for a Picnic Date

When you think of planning a romantic date during the day, more often than not, a picnic plays a role. A picnic basket loaded with the works—homemade sandwiches, cheese and crackers, grapes, a favorite bottled beverage, and a box of animal cookies for dessert—is a sure winning combination, especially when its contents are spread out over a checkered tablecloth.

When choosing the ideal spot for your next romantic picnic, be selective, be original, but most of all, be creative. Here are a few sites to consider:

* along the bank of a rippling stream, where you can skip rocks or hunt for crawdads together
* near a cascading waterfall after a pleasant hike into the woods
* in a meadow with a stunning view that can be reached only by horseback or four-wheel drive
* on the lawn of a historic site or county courthouse
* at a picturesque overlook near an ocean, lake, or pond

Different locations have a value and significance that is unique to each individual. Take the time to make your next picnic location one that'll be hard to forget.

 ## Teddy Bear Date

Many women and men still have a soft spot for teddy bears. Perhaps it's a fond recollection of their favorite doll growing up, or maybe they are avid Chicago Bears and Cubs fans and

# ⋆⋆ Spice It Up!

## Falling Star Kiss

Most loving couples remember their first kiss forever. Throughout this book are many creative suggestions for capturing the right moment for a first kiss. Here's one more: the Falling Star Kiss.

Whether the two of you are on a moonlit hike on a clear summer evening or sitting on the steps of your front porch at the end of your evening together, tell your date to gaze into the sky in search of the first falling star. When either of you sees one, use this as your signal to gaze into each other's eyes prior to a kiss.

The best thing about a Falling Star Kiss, other than the romantic memory you create, is that you get to make a wish. To increase the odds that your wish will come true, allow your star-gazing evening to last a while longer as you look for more falling stars—just possibly you'll create a lasting memory of the evening when the two of you first fell in love.

love anything that growls! In any case, a teddy bear date is just what they need.

Days before your scheduled date, mail your beloved a teddy bear greeting card with a note describing the theme of this upcoming date—teddy bears. On the appointed day, take your date to a novelty gift shop and buy a little teddy bear (or a Chicago Bears keychain!) to keep as a memento of the day. Or you could even arrange with the shopkeeper to surprise your date with a "free" teddy bear, which you purchased earlier in the week!

Be sure to incorporate the teddy bear theme into the rest of your date. You might sneak a pack of Gummi Bears into your date's coat pocket, play the song "Teddy Bear" by Elvis Presley on the car stereo, or watch a Bears or Cubs game at a local sports restaurant. If you're lucky, the date will end with a big bear hug!

 ## More Than Just a Dinner Date

A little teamwork from friends can make all the difference when masterminding the ideal creative date. Such is the case with the More Than Just a Dinner Date.

For this not-so-ordinary date, drive to a remote location, such as a cliff with an ocean view, a meadow, or a riverbank. As you get out of the car and begin walking down a trail, notice the surprised look on your unsuspecting date's face when a table adorned with a tablecloth, two fancy place settings, and candles comes into view. Not far from the table is a friend in a chef's hat, who is warming up the grill. This friend will play a triple role as chef, waiter, and entertainer for this occasion. Once dinner has been ordered, cooked to perfection, and served, your friend will smoothly bring out a guitar and begin to entertain you with some romantic acoustic sounds.

Unbeknownst to your date, another friend across the way in the nearby shrubs has been secretly taking candid pictures of this entire date using a telephoto lens. Later that evening, when you return home to watch a rented movie, place the photos (which have been developed at a one-hour photo shop and dropped off at your home by your friend) in the center of your coffee table for your date to discover!

# CHAPTER 3

# SPORT AND LEISURE DATES

**Y**ou don't have to be the athletic type to enjoy sport and leisure dates. Whether you're a serious sports enthusiast or simply a recreational runabout, there are countless ways to be creative with your favorite sporting or outdoor activities. Even if you are not the get-out-and-go type, you may find some of the date ideas in this chapter hard to resist.

Although sports and dating don't seem like natural partners, there are actually plenty of athletic and not-so-athletic activities that lend themselves nicely to dating relationships. From exerting extreme physical activity to watching others exert themselves on TV, these dates are sure to get you in shape or at least inspire you to get out and move. As with any new sport, however, you may need to practice some of these dates before getting the hang of it. But after sampling a few of the dates in this chapter, you'll be well on your way to becoming a real dating pro, of the sport and leisure kind.

 ## Trailblazer Date

When was the last time someone told you to take a hike? Hopefully it wasn't on your last date! But seriously, a peaceful trek in the great outdoors is a splendid way to conclude a laborious week at work, particularly if you're with that special someone.

To "gear up" for this excursion, fill your backpacks with all the essentials: a canteen of water, granola bars, a camera, a compass, bug spray, and so on. Then scout out a quaint location where you can have lunch with the squirrels. Be sure to keep an eye out for the legendary Bigfoot or any other "wild animal" (including your date!) who just might blaze across your trail.

 ## Kentucky Derby Date

It's always a special feeling to come away from a date with a rose in hand. Imagine how wonderful it would be to come away smelling like roses, too! This could happen to you after a successful evening at the racetrack, betting on your favorite thoroughbreds.

Winning a $2 exacta, trifecta, or quinella is all it takes to collect a cash reserve that could not only pay for your evening out but also support future creative dates together. If betting is not your game, or if the stakes seem a little too high for your budget, then bring along a roll of nickels or a bag of peanuts with which you and your date can privately wager.

On your way home from the track, stop by a local playground and ride the kid's carousel. Or maybe there is even a real carousel in the area! Have a race of your own.

If you don't feel up to the racetrack, you can always watch the Kentucky Derby or some other horse race at home on television. Make some mint juleps or homemade iced tea with mint leaves and cheer on your favorite horse as it runs for the roses!

## Take Me Out to the Ballgame Date

If you enjoy spectator sports, then you must consider taking your date to one of America's greatest pastimes: a professional baseball game.

Purchase a couple of tickets in advance for the outfield bleacher seats. These are the best seats for catching a souvenir home run ball. Prior to the game, have a picnic lunch outside on the stadium lawn and watch the thousands of fans stream into the ballpark.

Once the game is under way, buy some peanuts and Cracker Jack caramel corn to enjoy as you get ready to sing "Take Me Out to the Ballgame" during the seventh-inning stretch. Be a super fan and try to start the Wave.

Even if you don't live near a professional ball club, consider a college or high school game. A Little League game could be a great time as well.

## Shoot-Some-Hoops Date

Lace up your sneakers, put on your headbands, and then dribble over to the schoolyard for a comical time of playing some basketball together. Have a free-throw shooting contest, try playing around-the-world, or challenge each other to a spunky game of one-on-one. Or create your own game by making up the rules as you go along, using your best moves on one another.

To provide inspiration, play a special-effects tape that includes a recording of a boisterous crowd cheering in the background. (These tapes can be found at most music stores.) Whether it is a warm summer night under the streetlights or a rainy day under an overhang, anytime is suitable for some "hoopin' fun."

## Tennis Pro Date

Here's a little "topspin" you can add to your next tennis date. Recruit or hire a couple of neighborhood kids for the afternoon to be your own personal ball retrievers. Have them positioned at the net, prepared to eagerly fetch your point-winning smashes as well as your poorly aimed shots. Feel what it's like to be pampered, just like the pros.

Between sets, have one of your little helpers "serve" up thirst-quenching drinks from the cooler, while the other fans the two of you with a towel to keep you cool and refreshed for your next set. Now that's service your date will "love" you for!

## Homerun Derby Date

If you could imagine Babe Ruth on a creative date, this would be it! A plastic bat and a Wiffle ball are all you need to make a big hit.

Take your date to the nearest neighborhood park for a slugging match. Take turns pitching the ball to each other and hitting as many home runs as possible over the swing set or any other obstacle that makes a good home run fence. After several innings of big-league batting, go to a Denny's restaurant for their Grand Slam Breakfast special. Loser buys!

# ★ Spice It Up!

### Cracker Jack Surprise

Buy a box of Cracker Jack caramel corn and carefully open it up, replacing the original prize with a special prize of your own. Some ideas: two concert tickets, passes to the zoo, a friendship bracelet, a poem, a ring. Reseal the box as best as you can (make sure you leave no signs of tampering). Then, sometime during your date, whether it be on a picnic, at a baseball game, or at the movies, share your box of Cracker Jack candy and allow your date to discover the prize. This could make for a great photo moment!

 **Mini-Triathlon Date**

Comb the sports page for the next scheduled mini-triathlon in your area, and begin training together for this fun but challenging endurance event. Set up a training schedule and meet often for workouts. Or organize your very own triathlon just for the two of you. Plan a course to swim, bike, and run, designating an agreed-upon distance for each event.

Don't let bad weather keep you from enjoying time together. If the weather outdoors isn't cooperating, simply bring your mini-triathlon indoors to your health club, where you can swim in the pool, ride on the stationary bicycles, and run on the treadmills. Be creative with the rules. Add other activities, such as aerobics class, stair climbing, or rowing. Build in a handicap system, if necessary, to keep it competitive.

Before you begin your event, take a moment to predict what your finishing times will be. Whoever comes closest to the prediction is the winner. (No looking at your watches!)

## Buckaroo Date

Rodeos can be very exciting to watch, and best of all, you don't have to reside in the Wild West to attend one. Many cities across the country host professional rodeos at their indoor sports arenas, and chances are there's probably one coming soon to your neck of the woods.

Whether you're a city slicker or a country bumpkin, come dressed in your denims, cowboy hats, and boots and watch the cowboys "yee-haw" as they get bucked off their broncos. Cheer on the cowgirls as they compete against the clock while racing their horses around the barrels. When you get a hankerin' for some grub, shimmy on over to a western grill for some chow and a foot-stompin', hand-slappin' time of two-stepping and country line dancing.

## Sports Extravaganza Date

To make this a marquee event, sit down with your date and make a list of the sport and recreational activities you both enjoy the most. From your list, plan a Sports Extravaganza Date itinerary that charts a full day of exciting sporting events and activities. An example:

* Morning: Go in-line skating; play Frisbee in the park.
* Afternoon: Visit the health club for a Jacuzzi and a fresh fruit smoothie.

⁎ Evening: Go horseback riding; play a round of miniature golf; have dinner at a sports-themed restaurant.

Whichever activities end up on your list, keep your sense of spontaneity. Don't feel as though you must adhere to your original list of activities if something more exciting comes along.

Here are some additional ideas you may want to include in your Sports Extravaganza Date itinerary:

⁎ Hit a bucket of golf balls at the driving range.
⁎ Play horseshoes in the park.
⁎ Raft down the river.
⁎ Play racquetball.
⁎ Visit the batting cages.
⁎ Participate in an aerobics class.
⁎ Play table tennis.
⁎ Take a spin on the go-carts.
⁎ Watch a sports channel.
⁎ Go bowling.
⁎ Watch a rented sports movie.

 ## Scenic Run Date

If you run on a regular basis, you know how monotonous it can be to plod along the same course day in and day out, never experiencing much change in scenery. If the route you and your date have favored in the past seems to change only when the seasons do, then it's time to consider the Scenic Run Date.

Follow each other in separate cars to the place you plan to end your run. Once you've both arrived, leave your car there, and go together in your date's car along a picturesque route for whatever distance you desire to run.

After a quick pre-run stretch, start your one-way journey back to the first car, where, unbeknownst to your date, you have hidden a special post-run surprise in the trunk (a picnic basket with lunch inside or a jogging survival kit complete with bottled water, energy bars, fruit, sun block, and bandages for blisters).

Enjoy new scenery with each stride you take, knowing that you'll never have to retrace your route. With the Scenic Run Date, each time out is a new and exciting running experience.

 ## Moonlight Fishing Date

You don't have to be an expert angler to hook your date on this idea. After the sun has set for the evening, load the truck with your fishing gear. Then drive your date to a nearby pond for a moonlit fishing excursion. Have stashed in the shrubs two folding chairs, a card table, a picnic basket full of goodies, and some chopped wood you can use to build a cozy fire later. And don't forget the insect repellent, unless you want a less-than-pleasant memento of the occasion!

Once you've set up camp, toss your baited lines into the water and wait with anticipation for the first bite (even if you know the pond has no fish). In the meantime, roast some marshmallows over the open fire and make s'mores with chocolate bars and graham crackers.

# ESPN Sports Spectacular Date

When watching your favorite professional sports teams and stars in action, there's nothing as exciting as being there live among the throngs of energetic fans cheering your team to victory. However, it's not every day that couples can afford the rising costs associated with such an event (transportation to the venue, parking, tickets, hot dogs and drinks, souvenirs, and so on). Watching the game on television is simply not the same—unless, of course, you make it the ESPN Sports Spectacular Date.

For this date to transpire, consider the following essentials:

* The venue: your living room (parking is free)
* The medium: your big-screen TV and ESPN programming (no tickets required and great commentary)
* The food: an indoor wiener roast in your fireplace or woodstove (accompanied by a great supporting cast of your favorite condiments and beverages)
* The audience: you and your date (a winning combination)
* The twist: you and your date root for opposite teams (each of you can come clothed in that team's memorabilia)

To liven up the game, create your own "game(s) within the game" by making up the rules ahead of time. A few zany examples might include:

* The person whose team wins gets treated to a postgame victory dinner at a frilly restaurant. Loser pays.
* The person whose team scores the most touchdowns (baskets, runs, goals) in a designated time period gets a 10-minute massage for each touchdown. For instance, a 10-minute neck massage, a 10-minute back massage,

# ★★Spice It Up!

## A Clever Way to Ask Out a Guy

Sometimes a woman feels awkward asking a man out on a date, especially when it has traditionally been the man's duty to initiate a date. One subtle technique is to acquire a pair of advance tickets to an event you know the guy is interested in—a ballgame, for instance. Then ask the man out by saying, "I know you've played ball before, and I'd like to go with someone who knows something about the game. Would you care to join me?" Most men will be flattered and will take pride in knowing that they may be instrumental in making your experience at the ballpark more meaningful and fun.

and a 10-minute foot massage, in that order, for three touchdowns.

✳ If your team wins by a shutout, your date washes your car.

To spice things up a little, play a word game for kisses. Designate a particular word, name, or phrase that, when uttered over the airwaves, signals that it's time for a kiss. For example, assume that you have chosen the phrase *first down* as your indicator to give one another a kiss. Whenever you hear the ESPN commentator say, "He's just short of the first down" or "It's first down and goal-to-go," you give each other a kiss. You both could really roll up the yardage with this kissing game.

## Tailgater Date

Is the big game sold out again? Are the only available tickets those you can't afford? If so, worry no more. Round up your date, dress up in your school or team colors, and take a road trip to the stadium parking lot for the Tailgater Date.

No need to splurge for tickets, because you'll be watching this game on your portable TV or listening to it on your radio (be sure to stock up on batteries beforehand). You'll definitely be around the action, and your only cost is the price of admission—for parking! It's the next best thing to being there; the only difference is you're just outside the stadium.

Park next to an enthusiastic group of tailgating alumni or die-hard fans and do your best to join in on the pregame, half-time, and postgame festivities. Mingle with the multitude of fans in the parking lot grilling their grub over portable barbecues. Conjure up a few conversations with alumni and sing a bar or two of your favorite school fight songs. Walk around the parking lot to observe how the veteran tailgaters celebrate. Join in on a football toss to pass the time.

When it's time for the game to begin, pull your lawn chairs up to your portable TV and cheer your team to victory. After two quarters of play, enjoy the onslaught of fans as they return to their tailgates to freshen up with a half-time beverage or two and a healthful all-beef sausage dog.

Your tailgating experience may become so much fun that you decide to write a book about it, touring various stadiums (professional, major college, and others) in search of the greatest parking lot parties and the most spirited and loyal fans.

# CHAPTER 4

# SIMPLE AND FREE DATES

S trapped for cash again? Tired of looking under sofa cushions for a few spare dollars? If meager funds are putting a damper on your dating life, don't despair. In this chapter you will find many simple and easy date ideas that require no money at all!

But can a totally free date really be any fun? Of course! Remember, a successful date isn't measured by how much money you dole out or how elaborate your date itinerary is. On the contrary, a successful date is measured by such intangibles as the number of laughs you share, the quality of conversation, and the fun atmosphere you both create. So if the spare-coin compartment of your car once again turns up empty, realize it's time to make some real "change" and go on a date that's simple and free.

 **Photo Collage Date**

Carefully select about a dozen photos of your sweetheart that you have collected over the course of your dating relationship. Next, thumb through some old magazines and cut out words, phrases, and illustrations that affirm your date's qualities and character. Glue all your photos and snippets onto poster board to make a collage. Wrap it up and present it as a gift on your next date. Enjoy the heartfelt moment as you take the time to describe each entry and why you chose it. What a thoughtful way to honor your honey!

*Note:* This is an "affirmation" collage, not to be confused with an "insinuation" collage. Avoid the temptation to drop in an image that, subliminally or overtly, is snide or draws attention to a pet peeve or an annoying habit.

 ## Blockbuster Date

Lights, camera, action! A video camera and a small dose of humor are all you need to make this date a real blockbuster. Before you go out "on location," spend some time with your date writing a script for a series of short comedy scenes or commercials. Once your scripts are complete, go to a fun location (city park, shopping mall, downtown promenade, the beach) and take turns filming each other hamming it up in front of the camera.

Once your vision is on film, return home, make some popcorn, and put on your "critic hats" for the premier showing of your hit video. If you both agree that your production merits "two thumbs up," begin planning for your next box-office smash—*Blockbuster Date II: The Sequel.*

 ## Something Fun in the Trunk Date

Make a point of always carrying a variety of sporting goods, games, and other fun items in the trunk of your car. You never know when you'll need to pass some time between events or when you'll feel like getting out of the car for some recreation.

# ★★Spice It Up!

## Lollipop Surprise

If your date is a sucker for surprises, then here's one idea you have to try. At some point near the conclusion of your evening, reach into your coat pocket and remove a pair of lollipops, one for you and one for your date. When the lollipop wrapper is removed, your date will be puzzled to find a coupon wrapped around the sucker. The coupon bears the message "This coupon may be redeemed at any time for one fun and creative date with yours truly." Without saying a single word, you have just produced another opportunity to go out again!

Playing Frisbee or paddleball is a fun way to spend part of your afternoon. Keep a football in the trunk for those times when you two want to pull over to kick some field goals or throw each other a few passes (in more ways than one!). Other great items to pack in the trunk include two pairs of roller skates, a couple of putters and golf balls, a 500-piece jigsaw puzzle, a travel chess set, a basketball, a kite, and tennis rackets.

 ## Hometown Tour Date

Play tour guide for a day and give your date an up-close and personal look at the unique sights and local points of interest that make your hometown special. From the schools you attended while growing up to historic buildings and charming neighborhoods, don't leave anything out from your sightseeing tour. You can even include the places where you pulled ornery pranks on your friends and neighbors as a kid.

If you both happen to be from the same town, take turns being tour guide and share some new insights or unique points of interest about your town that your date may not be familiar with. It could be such things as how your town got its official name, or what famous person grew up in your town and what house they lived in.

After traipsing around town sharing your life stories, stop at the library and look through your town's historical records to learn a few new facts together or, if necessary, to verify your collective hometown knowledge, just in case there was some embellishment going on.

## Blooping Date

A body of water and a handful of rocks are all you need to make this date a splash. Meander down to a nearby lake or pond and instruct your date to throw a rock as high and as far out into the water as possible. As soon as the rock leaves the hand, you both begin kissing until you hear the rock go "bloop" into the water.

Continue to trade off, taking turns throwing a rock into the water and kissing until you hear the "bloop." When it comes time for your turn again, hold on to the rock and pretend that you really threw it! You then begin to kiss and kiss and kiss . . . listening for the "bloop" that never happens.

This date will make skipping rocks a thing of the past.

# ⭐Spice It Up!

## Leave a Note

One thoughtful but secretive way to express affection for your date is to leave a cute note in a coat pocket for him or her to discover later. Your message may say something like "Hi sweetie, have a great day!" or "Roses are red / Violets are blue / It was so much fun / being on a date with you." Write on your note whatever is appropriate for the occasion or for the feelings you wish to communicate. Other creative ways to leave a note include slipping it into a mailbox, a wallet or purse, or a medicine cabinet; taping it to a car's sun visor; and tucking it into a book as a bookmark.

 ## Beat Reporter Date

Develop a questionnaire covering a wide range of entertaining topics, then take it with you to a busy street corner or mall and conduct a poll or survey that would make the Gallup Organization envious. Together, ask your subjects questions such as "What was your most embarrassing moment on a date?" or "If you were stranded on an island, which three people would you want to be stranded with?" Be amused by the many interesting responses you receive from willing participants.

To take this date a step further, select a topic that is of special interest to you and your date and conduct some research together. Ideas for research topics might include favorite family traditions, best "small-world" stories, real-life miracles, and so on. After summarizing your survey findings, coauthor an article or human interest story and submit it for publication to your school or town newspaper.

##  Mystery Date

To demonstrate your imaginative side, make your next outing a mystery date of sorts by using clues or puzzles that, when solved, will reveal the next stage(s) of your date. For example, one clue might be "Yogi's downfall" (answer: picnic basket), indicating that you're about to embark on a picnic outing. A toy horse hidden in the car could be a clue that a horseback ride is in order.

Or, to score some points for creativity and thoughtfulness, make a homemade jigsaw puzzle for your date to piece together that will unveil the activity you have planned. It could be a postcard puzzle of a well-known area waterfall where you have planned to have a picnic. To keep it suspenseful, make sure the puzzle can't be solved until the last few pieces are put together.

## Make-a-Friend Date

For a great date designed to bring a little sunshine into a stranger's life, consider a date where the aim is to purposely seek out an individual to become acquainted with. Take some fresh-baked bread and a bouquet of handpicked flowers to the widow down the street. Strike up a conversation with a food service employee at the dorm cafeteria who's on a break. Visit an elderly person at a retirement home. You never know what common ground you might find or what small-world story is out there waiting to be exposed. Anticipate the feelings of gratitude that are certain to blossom among you, your date, and your new friend.

## Frisbee Golf Date

Frisbee golf can be played at almost any time, almost anywhere—a college campus, a city park, a neighborhood, the woods, or a camping trip. No reservations are needed!

If you choose a college campus as your course, consider making the first tee atop the student union steps. Designate each succeeding hole as you go along, adding your own hazards, strokes for par, and penalties. No etiquette is required here; however, a timely burst of laughter amid a stray toss is recommended.

Creating a target for each hole as you go along is just one of the many enjoyable parts of this game. Whether your target is the fire hydrant next to the home economics building for an easy par three, or a tricky par four that must bob and weave around a pair of oak trees before leaving a clear approach to the park bench, have fun as you complete your course. To make the game more challenging, impose a stroke penalty if the Frisbee lands in the bushes, on the sidewalk, or anywhere else you deem "out of bounds." Use your creativity and make up the rules as you go.

After concluding nine holes, take a "clubhouse" break at the campus deli or commons before continuing play on the "back nine."

## Bookstore Date

Bookstores provide plenty of amusement and literary fodder for hours of fun, laughter, and illuminating conversation. You can learn a lot about your date's personality, hobbies, and interests just by hanging out like a pair of "bookends." Bookstores are playgrounds where you can enjoy many simple and free "mini-dates" as you meander through the various sections.

Here are some creative ways you can make your bookstore date one worth writing home about:

* Check the store's activities calendar to see what events are on tap each month—perhaps a book signing by a local author, a leather-binding workshop, or a writing class. Participate in one or more of them.

* Cuddle up like a pair of bookworms and relax to the sounds of a local musician playing sultry notes on the sax or a few licks on the guitar.

* In the travel section, look through the maps and travel pictorials and plan a trip together.

* Visit the humor section, read joke books to one another, and see who can make the other burst out laughing first.

* Peruse the craft and hobby books and find a new activity that you can do together on a future date.

* In light of the "mini-date" theme, take turns reading a miniature book to one another for fifteen minutes.

* Regress to the days of your youth and visit the children's section. Share your childhood favorites. Sit in on a storytime reading by one of the store employees.

* Wander to separate ends of the bookstore with the goal of finding the most unusual, zany, or obscure book you can. Come together to share your findings and amazement at

how the books got published in the first place (and why you didn't think of the idea first).

* If the bookstore also sells music, preview the new releases and featured titles of your favorite artists.

No matter what your interests, you're sure to find a book that appeals to you and your date. When you do, find a cozy corner and read to one another.

 ## Good Samaritan Date

You get an indescribably wonderful feeling inside when you make a difference in the lives of others by graciously giving your time and talents to a noble cause. Whether you and your date volunteer to help out with a local charity or participate in a community service project, spending time together doing good deeds for others can result in a couple's most rewarding and memorable dates. In fact, most people will walk away from a date of this kind impressed that there's more to their date than they originally thought.

Here are some fun suggestions on how to be a Good Samaritan for a day:

* Assist an elderly couple with their yardwork. (Jump in the leaf piles a couple of times.)
* Volunteer to serve at a soup kitchen or homeless shelter.
* Spend an afternoon at a boys' or girls' club helping with planned games and activities.
* Choose a stretch of public road and pick up trash along the roadside—and maybe some wild blackberries too!
* Baby-sit for a couple who can't afford child care and who are long overdue for a date night out. Flip a coin for the diaper-changing duties.

* Find a family who doesn't have transportation and drive them around on a day of errands (getting their hair done, paying bills, grocery shopping, visiting relatives, and so on).
* Do some volunteer work at the animal shelter and try to find permanent homes for some of the puppies.

Once you're done helping the community, do a good deed for your date as well. Surprise your special someone by something as simple as doing the dishes or washing the car. It's amazing how far a kind gesture can go in a dating relationship.

 ## Public-Service Appreciation Date

Have you ever wondered what it would be like to be a police officer or a firefighter? Would you like to know what their job entails and what stories they have to share? How about National Park Service rangers—what's their job all about? Pick a public-service profession of special interest to you and your sweetie, and make a date to gain an appreciation for the men and women who serve and protect our communities and our state and national parks.

Go on a "ride-along" with a city police officer and learn about his or her job. Most cities have programs that let you reserve a block of time and get matched up with an officer for part or all of a shift.

Call your local fire department and schedule a guided tour of a fire station. See what it's like to live and work in a firehouse. Try on a firefighter's hat, hose something down, and ring the fire bell. Many stations will allow you to be timed at how fast you can get dressed in the fire-protective gear and slide down the fire pole. You may also pick up valuable tips about how to fireproof your home and other safety advice.

If you enjoy outdoor pursuits, such as hiking, camping, and bicycling, spend a day with a park ranger and learn what rangers do to protect our state and national parks. Gain valuable tips on hiking and camping safety, or go on a tour and learn about the wildlife and vegetation that's common to the area. Be sure to request a few hiking-trail maps for future outdoor dates. You and your date will walk away with a greater appreciation of nature, not to mention a few tidbits that you can share later with your friends.

Other public-service agencies you can contact in this spirit include your state's fish and game department, your state's forestry and fire protection department, and the U.S. Postal Service.

 ## Driving Instruction Date

Inevitably, there will come a time when you will be asked, or may willingly volunteer, to be a driving instructor for someone you know (such as your date) who needs a lesson or two on how to drive a stick shift (manual transmission). To keep this from becoming the Bumper Car Date or the Honk If You Hate My Driving Date, a country road or large empty parking lot is essential.

A date of this kind may offer important lessons needed for relationship building as well. Take trust, for instance: You have to trust that your date will keep the car on the road, and your date has to trust that you won't bill for chiropractic care because of the countless jerky starts and stops. Patience is another element of relationship building: You have to resist the temptation to ask your date, "Are we there yet?" after spending the first half-hour trying to get out of the driveway. Communication, teamwork, and forgiveness

# ★★Spice It Up!

## A Greeting Card for Any Occasion

Here's a simple idea to consider the next time you send your date a greeting card. Buy a card that is blank inside. In the left column, vertically spell the occasion (birthday, anniversary, etc.) that you are celebrating. Next, in conjunction with each vertical letter, horizontally write a word or phrase that describes a quality or an attribute that your date possesses. For example, "Happy Birthday":

**H**eaven sent
**A** blast to be with
**P**retty eyes
**P**ersonality that won't quit
**Y**outhful spirit

**B**est friend
**I**ncredibly fun
**R**eally fun
**T**houghtful
**H**appy Birthday to you
**D**id I mention really fun?
**A**wesome smile
**Y**ou're special

It's just one more way to creatively express your appreciation and affection.

---

are other relationship-building qualities certain to play a major role in such a roadway adventure.

To add a little romantic charm to this date, play the Stop Sign Game. When you're driving your date home, you will eventually come to a halt at a neighborhood stop sign. Once you do, keep the clutch in and give the car a little gas, as if there might be a transmission problem and your car is refusing to go into gear. When your date asks, "What's the problem?" you say, "Well, after 5 P.M. this car is programmed to remain at a stop sign until the driver receives a kiss!" Once your date reaches over and gives you a kiss, let out the clutch and drive on—to another stop sign, of course!

 ## People-Watching Date

Pick a busy location in the center of a city where a lot of folks hang out. Enjoy countless laughs as you make up stories about the people you see: where they are going, what they do for a living, and so on. Here are some fun topics to speculate about regarding the characters that cross your path:

* Upbringing: Big city or small town?
* Hair: Real or rug?
* Appetite: Vegetarian or carnivore?
* Underwear: Boxers or briefs?
* Endowments: WonderBra or implants?
* Hair: Natural or dyed?
* Profession: White-collar or blue-collar?
* Music preference: Classical or pop?
* Pet: Dog or cat?

The possibilities are endless! As you make up stories about each person, try to imitate what you think their voices sound like—high-pitched, nasal, deep, raspy, and so on. Before you know it, you'll have their whole (fictionalized) life mapped out. But be nice; some other couple may be doing the same to you.

## Money Not Included Date

As mentioned in this chapter's introduction, you don't have to be a cheapskate to go on a cheap date. Cheap dates aren't just for the struggling student on a college budget or the married couple with kids trying to make ends meet. Anyone can enjoy a no-cost yet meaningful date.

Although none of the dates in this chapter include money, the Money Not Included Date is one that involves the two of you working together, whether or not you're on a budget, to come up with ideas that promote quality time together using your collaborative creative talents. Here are some ideas to consider that won't cost a dime—a challenge in this day and age:

* Go to a warehouse wholesale store on the weekend to eat free food samples.
* See the city by walking around (or by riding public transportation, if it's free).
* Visit museums or art galleries that are free to the public.
* Window-shop at retail stores.
* Snag a previously read newspaper, and read the comics to each other or do a crossword puzzle together.
* Take a walk through a park or botanical garden.
* Attend a poetry reading at a local bookstore.
* If you live near the ocean, go for a walk on the beach and collect seashells or driftwood. Write each other's initials in the sand.
* Assemble a 1,000-piece jigsaw puzzle together.

A Money Not Included Date will prove that you can have a great time on a shoestring budget.

## Study Break Date

Give me a break! For anyone pulling an all-nighter to study for an exam or research project, a break can never come too often. Be a breath of fresh air by surprising your studious date with a well-deserved and well-timed break from the books.

Bring a couple of pairs of roller skates, one for you and one for your date, and skate through campus for a rejuvenating round of activity and laughter. Roll up to a bench for a pit stop and a snack and soda (which you remove from your backpack) before gliding back to the library or wherever your date was studying.

As a thoughtful gesture, stay with your date for a while, just long enough to help prepare for the upcoming quiz. Don't overstay your visit, however. It's best when you are the main attraction, not the main distraction!

Show your thoughtfulness by following up the next day and asking how your date felt he or she did on the quiz or assignment. If it was a success, you may want to demonstrate your academic interests (yeah, right!) by offering your Give Me a Break services for future cram sessions.

## Window-Shopping Date

Oh, what fun it is to dream! Just one day of window-shopping on Fifth Avenue in New York City or Beverly Hills' Rodeo Drive could have you and your date in R.E.M. bliss.

If you don't live near either of these high-profile fashion districts, do the next best thing and keep the dream-big spirit with a window-shopping spree in a spendy garment or jewelry district near your hometown. Dress up and play the "moneybags" role, trying on all types of expensive apparel and outrageously priced jewelry. Later, swing by the auto mall and see how good the two of you look and feel in a hot rod or a classic car.

As a matter of practicality, you may have as much fun, or more, window-shopping on your town's Main Street or at your local mall. Amuse yourselves by going in and out of all kinds of interesting stores, shops, and boutiques with character.

To transform this date into the "Splurge" variety, plan for your date to receive as a gift (within one week of the Window-Shopping Date) something he or she admired, tried on, or hinted at during the date, such as a diamond or pearl necklace or cuff links! Or keep to the "Simple and Free" theme by purchasing a modestly priced gift as a memento of your date.

# CHAPTER 5

# RAINY-DAY DATES

Is the inclement weather putting a damper on your dating barometer? If so, there's no need to fret. Some of the best dating moments can come while you're spending quality time with your honey in the warm and cuddly confines of the indoors, especially when there's a cozy fireplace crackling in the background.

Whether it's raining, snowing, or simply too hot to move, this chapter provides a downpour of creative dating ideas to enjoy when under cover, or, as in the case of the Liquid Sunshine Date, when there's no cover at all and you're creating memories splashing out in the rain. So grab your umbrella or don your warmest clothes, because things are sure to heat up when you incorporate some Rainy-Day Dates into your dating repertoire.

 **Musical Madness Date**

Give each other thirty minutes to write original lyrics to a familiar tune of your choice. Next, pick up a guitar or go to the piano and take turns singing your ditties to each other. If you can't carry a tune or you're still searching for your hidden musical talent, halt your search and sing it anyway! This will make it all the more fun.

For variety, team up and write a song together, taking turns composing one line or phrase at a time. Sing together in two-part harmony. If you dare, sing into a tape recorder and play it back. You'll be guaranteed a bundle of laughs.

If both of you can carry a tune farther than you can carry a piano, consider taking your show on the road to a karaoke bar or an audition with a community chorale.

 ## Liquid Sunshine Date

Raining again? Are you wasting another day at home wishing you could be outside enjoying the day with your sweetheart? If the rain is getting you down, then you need to "get down" in the rain! Pretend that it's a beautiful sunny day, and take a walk or go for a jog to the nearest tanning salon. Make a point of splashing your feet in every puddle en route. After a twenty-minute tanning session, return home for some hot chocolate and dry towels.

 ## Grocery Store Date

A trip to the grocery store is rarely thought of as something special to look forward to. In most cases, it's regarded as a necessary encumbrance, especially when the checkout lines are long and your stomach is growling like a grouchy old bear. But it's a different story when going to the market is part of a creative date!

You'll be surprised at the many laughs you'll share as you take turns pushing your cart up and down the aisles in search of the items from your shopping list. Just imagine what two people can learn from each other while shopping together. Your

# ★Spice It Up!

## Care Package

There are many occasions other than just being under the weather that merit receiving a care package. Working late hours to complete a work proposal, approaching the end of finals week, going away on a trip are just a few fitting occasions. It may even be a simple "Thank You" care package to show your appreciation for something. Or the care package could be for absolutely no reason at all. Include in your care package thoughtful items your date can relate to that are inexpensive, but useful—small in size, but big on fun—simple, yet imaginative.

As an alternative, you may team up with your date to prepare a care package for someone you both know who deserves a little TLC. Hand-deliver it in person, mail it with a thoughtful note, or simply leave it as an anonymous gift.

date might be able to teach you how to select a cantaloupe and determine whether it's a keeper. You might be a pro at picking out the freshest seafood. The possibilities are endless.

Now it's time to cook dinner! Go home, don your aprons, pop in an appropriate tape or CD, open a bottle of wine, and team up to concoct a gourmet dinner that would satisfy even the most discriminating palate.

## Airport Date

To most people, a major airport is a chaotic place where hurried travelers scamper feverishly to catch their flights or be herded into their respective gates like cattle waiting to be branded. To the creative dater, however, an airport serves as a prime indoor dating facility that offers a variety of exciting activities.

Begin your date by roving around the airport's concourse to do a little people-watching. Observe the many travelers scurrying from gate to gate. Strike up a conversation with a stranger on layover. Learn something new and interesting.

Next, have dinner in one of the airport's restaurants, making sure to request a table with a view of the planes landing and taking off. Or, if this is too pricey, bring your own snacks and sit near one of the large windows in the terminal. While you dine on your airport meal, talk about your dream vacation, or maybe plan a trip for the two of you to take one day. Afterward, take a moment to browse through the various gift shops, and consider buying each other a souvenir as a memento of your evening together.

## Learn-a-New-Skill Date

Another rainy day? Turn it into a rainy date. Spend a day with your date learning a new skill or activity from each other. There are many skills two people can learn from each other that are both useful and fun. For example, you can learn (or teach) how to:

* sew on a button
* cook a meal from scratch
* accessorize your clothes
* change or rotate a tire
* program a VCR
* plumb a sink

Fun but not so useful skills include learning how to:

* pluck your eyebrows
* darn a sock
* tie a cherry stem into a knot with your tongue
* belch out a sentence
* play tonsil hockey

Another angle to explore is to learn a skill or do an activity together that both of you are interested in but neither has experienced. Examples include learning to play a guitar, frame a picture, or refinish a piece of furniture.

 ## Plan-a-Dream-Trip Date

It doesn't cost anything to dream, and planning an imaginary trip to an island paradise or resort town is one way to assuage your dream-travel aspirations and bring you one step closer to making it a reality.

Choose a location to meet your date, such as a coffee shop, a bookstore travel section, or your living room floor. Spread out all of the maps, brochures, and travel guides that you each have resourcefully gathered for this occasion.

To further enhance your travel-planning evening, search together on the Web for travel companies that offer package trips to your favorite destination. Search for and print out a month-to-month calendar of interesting activities, such as concerts and luaus, that may be going on during the time of year that you imagine yourselves being there.

Let your fantasy bank account be your guide and assist you in determining the costs of airfare, cruises, hotel, food, souvenirs, and so on. If your trip is a cross-country adventure, then determine how many miles you'll be driving, the tourist attractions you'll be visiting, the places you'll lodge for the evening, and so on.

Bring your Plan-a-Dream-Trip Date one step closer to the real deal by pretending that you're really on the trip in the city or country you want to visit. For example, if your fantasy trip is a resort town in Mexico, wear a sombrero, play mariachi music in the background, make fresh guacamole and salsa, and sip on fruity tropical drinks. Set up the room with posters of the city (available from travel agencies), plaster brochures on the wall, and decorate accordingly.

# ★ Spice It Up!

## Chilly Message

There's nothing particularly unusual about a plain ol' ice cube, unless of course it is floating in your date's drink and has a written message frozen in it. As peculiar as this may sound, an ice cube with warm thoughts can quench the thirst of even the most discriminating beverage connoisseurs.

To create your chilly message, begin by writing a few short inspirational thoughts on thin strips of paper using indelible ink. Thoughts may include "You're cool," or "Our love is frozen in time." Cut the messages the same length as the ice cubes.

Next, fill an ice tray with water and let it freeze until partially frozen. Then remove the semi-frozen cubes and place the notes face down against the bottom of the cubes. Return them to the tray and re-freeze. After the cubes are frozen solid, put them into your date's glass and pour a drink, making sure the notes visibly float to the top. Your date will be astonished at your creative expression.

As a conclusion to your Plan-a-Dream-Trip Date, cut out pictures, words, and phrases from your trip-planning resources, paste them on a sealed jar, and put in your spare change. Maybe this trip will become a reality sooner than you think!

 ## Your Own Private Spa Date

Spoil each other with a hair-raising home salon and spa retreat. Take turns washing and conditioning each other's hair, making sure to include a scalp massage prior to the rinse. For effect, consider adding a little spray-in instant hair color.

After you've had a go-round or two on each other's dos, transition to the spa phase of your date. Put on a pair of comfy slippers, play some relaxing music, light a few aromatherapy candles or incense, and get ready for a night of pampering. This first step is the facial. For many of you guys, this will be an all-new experience! While your face is enjoying a foaming mousse mask and a cucumber eye treatment, you can be further spoiled by a simultaneous hand soak and massage. Finally, you can experience the joys of having your broken nails fixed and your cuticles pushed back. (Just don't tell the fellas.) Take a break and refresh yourselves with tall glasses of ice water with lemon slices or mint sprigs.

Next, it's the woman's turn to be pampered. After what will probably be a bungled, novice attempt by the guy to emulate the hand-soak and manicure experience, he can take a shot at applying some mood-changing polish to your nails.

Once you are both pampered, clean, and relaxed, curl up on the couch and listen to the music as you drift off to sleep.

## Games People Play Date

The next time bad weather has you tethered indoors, keep from getting bored by taking your date to get a "board"—a board game, that is—at the nearest toy store. Dash across town to pick up your date for a cozy afternoon at your sheltered abode. On your way back, make a pit stop at the toy store and lose yourselves among the thousands of toys and games that will take you back to the days of your youth.

Laugh and learn more about each other as you wander up and down the aisles reminiscing about your childhood and the games you once played. Before you leave this toyland paradise, pick up an old favorite to play with for old times' sake once you've returned home. Maybe something like Candyland, Chutes and Ladders, or Twister.

Games to avoid playing as part of a rainy day date, or any date for that matter, are the "mind" games. You know the ones. How about the "I'm going to play hard to get" game or the "Guess why I'm mad at you, because I'm not telling" game.

If cash is tight, just take home some ideas and create your own board game. All you need is some cardboard and felt-tip pens. For game pieces use such odds and ends as spare coins, buttons, and earrings. Draw your game board on the cardboard and make up your own rules. If you're really daring, play for real kisses instead of fake money.

## Create-a-Pizza Date

Bad weather can certainly put a damper on your plans for an outdoor date, but one thing it's not likely to dampen is your appetite. Good weather or bad, you've gotta eat. So "weather" or not, food here we come!

A complement to any indoor activity is to create your own pizza together. It's easy, and, best of all, it requires a team effort. The ready-to-use pizza dough and sauce provide the basics. The fun comes when you go to the store to select your toppings (olives, 'shrooms, pepperoni, etc.). Try some new toppings you never considered before, such as pineapple, asparagus, potatoes, or even candy. See who can come up with the most outrageous yet delicious creation. Whatever you do, be sure to leave out the onions—this is a date, after all.

 **Malling Date**

Not to be confused with siccing your pit bull on the neighbor's pesky cat, this date is an assault on the local shopping mall. Whether the temperature outside is a scorching-hot 100-plus degrees or below zero with a wind-chill factor that takes your breath away, your local mall can provide a comfortable, safe harbor for a creative date.

You can have hours of fun here without spending a lot of hard cash—really! What you will get are a lot of hard laughs. Here are some ideas to make your time at the mall nothing short of fabulous:

* Try on fun jewelry, accessories, and clothes, including some you'd never imagine wearing in public.
* Drop each other hints or ideas for a birthday or holiday gift.
* Take silly pictures together in a photo booth.
* Have lunch in the food court. Afterward, grab a mocha or coffee and people-watch.
* Buy some cheap earrings and get your ears pierced free.
* Go to the furniture section of a department store and sit on the lounge chairs next to the televisions.

* Strike up a conversation with a stranger.
* Go for a ride on the carousel.
* Drop in to a specialty or novelty store and relax in a chair-massage lounger to restore your energy before taking another loop around the mall.
* Visit one of the mall's card shops and read greeting cards to one another.

The possibilities are endless. At some time during your date, make a point of visiting a sunglass store to try on some cool shades. Just before you slip on a pair, tell your date that you have something caught in your eye. Ask your date to draw near and take a peek to see what it might be. As your sweetie comes up close to examine your eye, sneak a kiss and say, "Ah, thanks. I see much better now." Works every time!

 ## Vintage Comedy Radio Show Date

Spend an evening together in front of the radio, just the way your grandparents did in the old days. Many hysterically funny comedy radio shows are on the air these days; just check your local AM frequency programming. After you listen to one of these with your date, mimic the style of the characters on the program. You'll both be doubled over with laughter. Some of the vintage shows can even be downloaded from the Internet.

You can also purchase recordings at a bookstore. Some entertaining personalities to consider for this date include Bill Cosby, Bob Newhart, Jerry Seinfeld, and Garrison Keillor. Hearing just a line or two from one of your favorite shows will have you in stitches.

## Picture-Perfect Date

A diversion from other photo-theme dates mentioned in this book is the Picture-Perfect Date. This date leads off with a photo-shooting frenzy at a quick-stop specialty photography store. Don't pay the big bucks for a professional photographer; instead, line up behind the kiddies and their moms, and put on a real show when it's your turn to be big kids in front of the camera. Bring several sets of clothes or props (hats, shades, etc.) to ensure a myriad of different looks. Anticipate the thrill of returning later in the afternoon to preview your prints.

Then the real fun begins. Decide how and what to do with your hilarious snapshots. Most quick-stop photo stores offer a variety of creative ideas for you to choose from. Certainly you can frame your creative portraits and keep them at your home or office, but also consider making a picture book or arranging a photo sculpture on a stand. Or have your photos transferred onto a dress tie, a mug, or a mouse pad.

The idea here is to do something out of the ordinary. This could include ordering key chains, pins, picture puzzles, or ornaments that bear your mug shots. You can also personalize note cards or make postcards with your own portraits and send them to your friends and family.

 ## Talent/No Talent Date

Each of us has been blessed with different gifts and abilities that make up part of who we are. Sharing these gifts is harder for some than it is for others, but it is an important part of the attraction process. Creating a forum where these gifts can be expressed is what the Talent/No Talent date is all about.

The aim of this date is to humor and amaze each other with your collective range of talents (hidden or otherwise). Letting your personalities shine through your talents is a great way to learn more about each other as well as pass the time on a rainy day.

Take turns impressing one another with your various talents. They could include the ability to play a musical instrument or a skill in the visual arts, such as drawing, painting, or origami.

If you claim to be in the No Talent category (which really is a talent, by the way), have fun showing off your unique, nontraditional skills and abilities: balancing a spoon on your nose, spinning a basketball on your finger, walking and chewing gum at the same time, and so on.

Here are some other Talent/No Talent ideas to consider:

* Speak a foreign language. Or make up a foreign language and convince your date it really is authentic.
* Play Chubby Bunny: See how many marshmallows (one at a time) you can stuff into your mouth and still be able to say "Chubby Bunny."
* Make your ears wiggle.
* Touch your nose with your tongue.
* Do a push-up with one arm only.
* Perform a few impressive card tricks.

For an encore sure to impress, perform the quarter trick. Bet a quarter that you can kiss your date without physically touching. Thinking for a moment, your date will conclude that this cannot be done and will agree, fully expecting to win the bet. At that very instant, plant a big kiss on your

# ⭐Spice It Up!

## Luck of the Draw

Write date ideas and thoughtful things you would like your honey to do for you on little sheets of paper. Have your honey do the same. Roll up your ideas like miniature scrolls and put them in a "dating jar." Take turns randomly drawing a scroll from the jar as often as you like.

Agree to include among your ideas some thoughtful treats, some fun and frugal dates, and a few splurges to share together. Decide how frequently you draw from the jar. Thoughtful treats could include bringing fresh flowers home every day for a week, receiving a one-hour back rub, or receiving a one-day "free from the kitchen" coupon. Fun and frugal dates could include an ice cream sundae and a weekend matinee, a favorite (inexpensive) meal cooked by your date, or a lunch meeting during the week. Splurges could include a spontaneous weekend getaway, a $100 shopping spree at your favorite department store, or a lavish night on the town to see a play, preceded by a romantic candlelight dinner at a fancy restaurant.

date. Then back off for a moment, flip your date the quarter, and say, "I lose!"

## Humor Me Date

Some dates can be ideal for breaking the ice or easing the tension that may occur from time to time during dating relationships. Such is the case with the Humor Me Date. It offers a "teachable moment" during which couples can learn more about each other while sharing some laughter at the same time.

Begin by allowing each other fifteen minutes to complete select sentences from a Humor Me Questionnaire that you've put together in advance. (See example below.) When you're finished, go back and forth sharing your answers to question 1, question 2, question 3, and so on.

### Humor Me Questionnaire

A funny thing happened when I . . .

. . . was in grade school.

. . . was learning to drive.

. . . played sports.

. . . tried to cook.

. . . got my first job.

. . . went on my first date.

. . . was on my last vacation.

. . . was at school.

### Other Questions

I got in big trouble when . . .

I laughed my hardest when . . .

My most embarrassing moment was . . .

My number one pet peeve is . . .

My greatest accomplishment is . . .

At the conclusion of this exercise, talk about how you feel about each other after sharing several moments of laughter together. You will both likely realize that humor can have quite a positive effect on a relationship, and that you just took one more step on the road to getting to know your date.

## Scrapbook Date

One of the greatest benefits of dating is the lasting memories you create together. Every dating couple has a story to tell, and one of the most creative ways to tell that story is through a well-constructed scrapbook. Give it a theme, such as "Over the Years" or "Our Trip to . . . ". On the next rainy day, meet to record your memories of previous dates.

Let's assume that on one particular date you took a weekend excursion to Seattle. Here are some essential scrapbook-worthy items to collect and bring home: maps, programs, postcards, receipts, matchbooks, souvenir dinner placemats, ticket stubs, and anything else that will tell your story. Candid photos of all the places you visited (Pike Place Market, the Space Needle, a Washington State Ferry, the Mariners' Safeco Field) will help bring your story to life.

Together with your date, rummage through your collection of photos and memorabilia and organize your scrapbook chronologically. Important items to have on hand to help make this date a success include photo labels to title each photo, mounting sleeves, photo corners, stencils, stamps, decals, mounting adhesive, construction paper, scissors, and so on. You can get them all at a crafts supply store.

Enjoy the moments you spend developing your memory book and reflecting on the significant times you have shared. As a finale, set aside thirty minutes each and write a personal summary, poem, or travel review to include at the end of your scrapbook that will make you want to look back on the trip it chronicles for years to come.

# CHAPTER 6

# OUTDOOR DATES

**M**any dates can be enjoyed outdoors, but some in particular call for nature's playground to serve as host. Tandem bike riding, flying a kite, or going on a frolicsome scavenger hunt for two—planning an outdoors date can be exciting and fun.

Even if you're not the outdoorsy type, there are numerous date ideas that may just change your mind. There's everything from picnicking and stargazing to taking a Sunday drive along a country road. All are outdoor activities that don't require much exertion and promote a stress-free event.

For awesome times under the sun—or under the moon, for that matter—simply peruse this chapter. The many nature-oriented activities within will be sure to cast some light on your dating relationship.

 **Tandem Bike Ride Date**

Double your pleasure with a tandem bike ride excursion that you will surely want to write home about. Rent a tandem bicycle at the nearest bike rental shop for several hours of riding fun. Tour up and down a beach or along a lakefront promenade, taking in all the sights while getting a little exercise along the way. Observe the array of folks looking on with curiosity and envy.

After you've worked up a thirst, stop for an ice-cold lemonade before cruising back to where you began. On the way back, plan to stop at a city park to snack on some cheese and crackers that you have stored in your backpack. Save a few of your leftovers and feed the squirrels that have so generously allowed you to drop in for a rest stop where they call home.

## Modeling Date

Load your camera with a roll of film, head to the nearest park, and alternate taking pictures of each other posing as models. Shoot in a wide variety of locations and poses. Take some candid and off-the-wall shots as well, so you can anticipate the good laughs you'll have when you get the pictures back.

Take your film to a one-hour photo shop to be developed. During the hour wait, take some time to "develop" a few areas of your relationship as well. For every exposure on your roll of film, be it 12, 24, or 36, try to learn an equal number of new things about each other: hobbies, interests, favorite foods, movies, pet peeves, and so on.

Once the pictures are ready, bring them home and make mini–photo albums to exchange as gifts.

## Fly-a-Kite Date

Make a date to assemble a homemade kite together. A few wooden dowels, some lightweight nylon material, glue, and string are all you'll need to make this date "take off." Come up with a creative theme, emblem, or slogan that has meaning to both of you, and decorate your kite as colorfully and creatively as you can, incorporating your symbolic message.

Once your kite's construction is complete, and when the afternoon wind conditions are ideal, take it to the park for its inaugural flight. Run with it and watch it soar through the sky. After you have each taken a few turns directing your kite, tie it to a solid object and have a picnic together as your engineering marvel, surely destined for the Smithsonian's National Air and Space Museum, hovers overhead.

## Treasure Hunt Date

Buy your date a present and wrap it up in an old box. Next, take it to the beach and bury it safely in the sand. Draw a treasure map. Leave the map in a conspicuous place where your date can easily find it.

Set out with your date to hunt the hidden treasure, pretending for as long as you can that you have no idea where the map came from. Once you've followed all the clues and have arrived at "X" marks the spot, begin digging together for the lucky treasure. Your date will be overcome with delight after learning that it was you who masterminded this mystery.

## A Date at the Zoo

There's something special about a zoo that attracts dating couples. It's here that you can spend hours of fun watching the different animals, birds, and reptiles living peacefully in their exotic habitats. Maybe you'll be inspired to coil up like a couple of baby boa constrictors.

Be sure to bring your camera and take pictures of the baby tigers wrestling playfully or the monkeys swinging from tree

# ★★Spice It Up!

### Soda-in-the-Tree Surprise

On your next walk, run, or bike ride through the neighborhood park, make a timely rest stop under a shady tree and amaze your date with the thirst-quenching soda-in-the-tree surprise.

As you approach the shady tree under which you plan to relax, say to your date, "I sure could go for an ice cold soda right now. How about you?" Assuming your date concurs, immediately reach into the hollow portion of the tree trunk and pull out two cans of soda chilled on ice. What a surprise it'll be for your date to learn that you had placed the drinks in the tree just moments before you met up together.

to tree. Have someone snap a few photos of you and your date feeding peanuts to the elephants. To save some money and to avoid eating the zoo cafeteria food, pack a brown-bag lunch and some drinks and have a picnic while you watch all the families enjoying the zoo animals.

 ## Night-Putting Date

Have your next dinner at or near a local golf course—the perfect setting for a round or two of night putting. Following dinner, retrieve two putters and some golf balls from the trunk of your car, then entertain each other with a post-dinner interlude of putting on the practice green. Putt against each other for a nickel a hole, or perhaps play each hole for a kiss! Be sneaky and secretly drop a small gift (earrings or movie tickets, for instance) in the hole for your date to discover when he or she retrieves the ball.

## Green Thumb Date

You can draw many parallels between dating relationships and gardens: Both require patience and take time to grow. If left unattended, they will dry up and wither. Hardships may cause temporary pain, but in the long run, a little "pruning" will ultimately yield much fruit.

Hence the Green Thumb Date is particularly apt. Choose a plant, shrub, fruit, or flower that is most symbolic of your dating relationship. Make a date to plant and cultivate it together: perhaps a happy grouping of sunflowers, a fast-growing ivy, or a humorous Chia Pet. Whichever option you choose, may you enjoy the wonder of seeing your plant life, as well as your dating life, grow abundantly.

As an alternative, take a drive to a location that boasts the county's, state's, or world's largest tree or plant form—perhaps a Sitka spruce, a redwood tree, or a mulberry. Gather some seedlings from the ground in which the tree is rooted. Take them home, plant them on your property, and watch them take root and grow. If you don't have any available garden space, don't worry. Plant your seeds, bulbs, nuts, or kernels along the side of a nearby country road.

## Date of Antiquity

Great fun, cheap admission, and lots of laughter are just a few benefits of spending time together on a date at an outdoor swap meet or antiques show. After browsing around together for a while, separate with the goal of having each person find the most unique, silliest, or ugliest item and buy it as a gift for the other person. Put a dollar limit on the gift—perhaps $3 to $5. Learn how amazing and hideous some of the "junk" you wade through can be. Regardless of what your date thinks of the item you buy, it'll surely make for a nice memento of a fun day.

On a more surreptitious note, while browsing together, make a note of the item your date seemed to find most beautiful or inspiring—probably one that he or she made a point of showing to you. After the date is over, go back to the show and buy that item for your honey, keeping it a secret for days, weeks, or months until the perfect occasion arises to present it as a gift. Now that's romantic!

 ## Tune-up/Auto Detail Date

Here's a date idea that not only will keep your car tuned up and looking spiffy, but will also keep your dating relationship revved up and in good working condition. Dress in your grubbiest clothes and devote a sunny afternoon to giving each other's cars a little general maintenance and detailing.

Help each other with the maintenance chores. This could be a great opportunity to learn some auto basics that are essential to maintaining your car and your own safety. Possibilities include checking and changing the oil, inspecting and topping off the transmission fluid, and checking the tires' air pressure. After the tune-up phase of this date, peel off your grubbies and get into your shorts for the car wash and auto detail phase.

To make this date complete, be sure to follow these recommended steps:

### Tune-up/Auto Detail Inspection List

✔ Check the tire's air pressure.

✔ Crank up the tunes and do a car-dance boogie.

✔ Rotate the tires.

✔ Smear grease on each other's faces.

✔ Wash and wax the car.

✔ Snap each other with a wet towel.

✔ Clean the car's interior.

✔ Put another layer of suntan lotion on each other.

✔ Install a new air freshener.

✔ Install a breath mint in each other's mouths.

✔ Inspect the windshield wipers.

After a fun day of mechanical work, cleanup, and horsing around, hop in one of the cars (a convertible would be best) and go for a spin around town. Consider picking up some fast food at a drive-up window before heading off to a drive-in movie.

This date could also be easily modified to become the Tune-up/Boat, RV, or Motorcycle Detail Date.

 ## Scavenger Hunt Date

Scavenger hunts are adventurous and fun, and they don't always have to be experienced in large group settings. The Scavenger Hunt Date offers all the excitement and thrills of a traditional scavenger hunt, but it also includes a few unique twists and variations sure to make this discovery-theme date a real treasure.

# ★★ Spice It Up!

## Creative Activity Puzzle

Even if you're not the artistic type, this idea can still be a lot of fun. Draw a picture that represents what you will be doing on your date (a picnic basket or a bicycle, for instance). You can also use a photograph you've taken or an image from a magazine, a postcard, or the like. Cut the picture into jigsaw-puzzle pieces. Every day prior to the big event, mail your date two or three pieces of the puzzle. As each day goes by and your date slowly assembles the puzzle, the plan for the special event will begin to unfold. To keep it suspenseful, make sure the puzzle can't be solved until the last few pieces are added.

Begin your hunt with a pre-chase planning meeting at your house. Create a Top 10 list of interesting items that you want to pursue or places you seek to find. Make some of them simple and easy, and others super-challenging.

Unlike the goal of a traditional scavenger hunt, which is to find clues leading you to a final destination, the goal of this adventure is to see how many items from your list you can find. Here are some ideas:

* Find a hubcap lying on the side of a road.
* Spot someone with unusual-colored hair.
* Meet someone who has lived in Alaska.
* Look in the classified section of the newspaper under "Lost and Found" and see if you can find what's missing.
* Think of a place you've often heard of but have never been to (an ice cream shop known for great waffle cones, for

instance), and find it without the assistance of a phone book or map.

✱ Peruse a magazine for an item that appeals to either of you (a Yankees baseball cap or a white PT Cruiser, for instance), and see if you can find one just like it. (Just locate it; don't buy it, of course.)

✱ Looking for that matching candleholder? This could be your lucky day. See if you can find the mate at a garage sale, swap meet, or department store.

✱ On a paper bag, list things you might find at a park (pine cones, feathers, maple leaves, candy wrappers, and so on) or things that you might expect to see there (a squirrel, a couple holding hands, someone going down a slide, and so on). Don't leave the park until you have gathered or spotted all the items from the list.

Give yourselves a time limit to discover the items on your list. Together, develop prize categories based on the number of items found from your list, and award yourselves accordingly.

**Sample Prize Categories**

| Items Found | Prize (Related to your scavenger hunt list) |
| --- | --- |
| 1–4 | Tasty famous waffle cones |
| 5–7 | Baseball cap and a PT Cruiser test drive |
| 8–10 | Matching candleholder or a trip to Alaska! |

## Ice-Blocking Date

Here's a thrill-seeking date adventure that'll surely bring a chill to your spine. On a warm spring or summer night, go to the grocery store and buy two large ice blocks—one for you and one for your date. Next, find a grassy knoll and partake in an evening of ice blocking. It's actually quite simple and lots of fun. Climb to the top of the knoll with your ice block. Place a towel on the ice, sit on it, and then slide down the hill as if you were sledding. Once you get the hang of it, race each other to see who can reach the bottom first. If you get really good, put your blocks together and try sliding down in dual fashion. Be sure that both of you wear pants, and bring plenty of towels with you to dry off. Whatever you do, don't go on this date during the day. You wouldn't want the sun to cut your date short by melting the ice.

 ## Sunday Drive Date

Here's a date that's suitable for all dating couples, whether they are single, married, and/or with kids. Whatever your dating status, there's something peaceful about packing up the car with a few essentials (picnic lunch, ice chest with sodas, suntan lotion and towels, map, a good book, butterfly net, your dog Skippy, and so on) and heading out for a Sunday drive to an unknown destination.

For some, this date may take you back to the times of your youth, when a Sunday drive with the family was as common as watching football games on TV or attending soccer practice is today.

Begin this date with a stop at the filling station to gas up (this doesn't mean with chilidogs from the minimart) and then head on out. Find a country road with scenic views and begin your exploration. Feel free to drive more slowly than the speed limit, taking in all of nature's beauty along the way. Take your time and enjoy as much nature as possible. Strive to remove yourself from the stresses of life or the pressures of work that may await you on Monday.

Here are a few suggestions for places to see and pit stops to make along your way:

* Find a country school and go for a swing on the playground.
* Stop and read every historical marker you come across.
* Explore an old logging road not found on the map.
* Pull off the road and hike a trail down to a stream below. Skip a few rocks in the water (but only if there are no fishermen about!).
* If it's a hot day, wade in the water to cool off (watch out for the crawdads), or find a large rock where you can sit and work on your tans.
* Find a train trestle and walk across it.

The leisurely Sunday drive may just become a tradition that your kids will fondly look back on some day.

# ★★ Spice It Up!

## The Art of Being a Good Listener

It takes a substantial effort to be a good listener. It's tough for some to realize that part of good communication in any relationship is knowing when to keep your ears open and your mouth shut.

Make a point of learning about your date's hobbies, interests, and favorite things (foods, colors, TV shows, etc.). Then incorporate many of these preferences into your future dates together. For example, if you know her favorite candy is chocolate and her favorite flowers are daffodils, present her with a bouquet of hand-picked daffodils and a chocolate truffle(s) the next time you pick her up. Similarly, if you learn that he's a big fan of country and western music, have his favorite country songs playing in the background when you've invited him over for dinner.

Whatever you do to demonstrate that your listening skills are "tuned in," remember that the thought counts more than the cost.

 **Sparking Date**

On your next outdoor date that takes place at night, whether it be a romantic moonlit canoe ride on a lake, a hike on the bluffs, a visit to the drive-in, or even a zany, nighttime Bigfoot-hunting expedition, be sure to bring along a pack of Wint-O-Green LifeSavers candy so you and your date can lighten things up with fun "sparking" experiments.

What is "sparking"? When you bite down on a Wint-O-Green LifeSaver in the dark, it creates a little spark in your mouth. Try it some time; it really works! After you both have made sparks with your candy, create a few sparks of your own with each other's lips. Breath mints have never been so much fun. Be sure to bring a couple of packs!

# CHAPTER 7

# DOUBLE DATES

ating with other couples has many benefits. Not only can you gain greater insight into your date's personality, but you can also have some hilarious times together that can only be spurred by having more than just two people participating. When a group of creative thinkers gets together, there's no telling how remarkable or spontaneous a date may become. In many cases, it's the date-planning activities beforehand that can steal the show, becoming just as much fun and outrageous as the date itself. In this chapter, you will discover firsthand how couples can join forces in planning the utmost in creative dates. These duet-date ideas may ignite the spark you need to get the creative ball rolling for your next get-together!

 **Dazzling Dessert Date**

Surprise your dates with a post-dinner scavenger hunt that leads them to a fun location for a creative dessert.

To begin, hand your dates the first clue and inform them of their scavenger hunt mission. As they begin their search, hustle back to the parking lot and unload the necessary equipment from the trunk of your car. Transport it to the creative location and set up the surprise dessert—chocolate fondue. Cut up some fresh apples, bananas, strawberries, and marshmallows, then melt chocolate over a Sterno fire for dipping.

In the meantime, your dates will be scurrying to find the final clue that might read something like this:

*Back to the start where you began,*
*take a walk down the sidewalk strand.*
*Near the closest lifeguard tower*
*awaits the dessert we're about to devour.*
*Dessert will be fine, but not to compare,*
*to the incredible time we're sure to have there.*

On arrival, your dates will be impressed by the wonderful gourmet dessert you have delicately prepared. Take delight in your dessert and enjoy many laughs as your dates recount their triumphs and follies during their clue-finding journey.

 ## Video Scavenger Hunt Date

Have you ever wanted to sing at a karaoke lounge in front of a live audience? What about selling fruit on a street corner? Here's your chance to watch yourself and your friends get wild and crazy on camera! This date is especially suitable for a large group.

After your guest couples have arrived, have couples divide up into groups of four, equipped with a video camera and a list of activities they must capture on tape to complete the video scavenger hunt. Once everyone has fulfilled all the requirements (or the designated time limit is up), meet back at your home for snacks and the eagerly anticipated viewing of your creative video antics. Award prizes in categories such as "funniest," "most creative," "most embarrassing," and "most original."

## Country Barn Dance Date

"Find your partner, give her a swing, promenade home with the pretty little thing." A fun-filled date of square dancing or a rollicking time of two-stepping, combined with a gathering of friends at Farmer Jones's ranch for a country and western barn dance and barbecue makes for an evening that even the cows will want to come home for.

To initiate this country hoedown, the men get together early in the day for a male-bonding time of barn cleaning, dance-floor decorating, music mixing, and barbecue-pit prepping. In the meantime, the women "doll up" for this special occasion in their finest western garb.

Once all the final preparations have been made, the men can go around house to house in Farmer Jones's flatbed truck laden with hay, rounding up their dates for the evening. Once everyone has been gathered up, you can all enjoy a spin or two through town before heading out to the ranch for an unforgettable time.

 ## A Date with Mom and Dad

Have you ever considered going out on a double date with your parents? If not, why not take them out for a special night on the town? Moms and dads can be a lot of fun, especially when they're reminded of their times together in their dating youth.

Throughout the evening's agenda, include a few activities from their era to bring back some warm thoughts of their past. For example, play a Glenn Miller or Frank Sinatra tape in the car, rent *Gone With the Wind*, have dinner at a '50s restaurant, spend the evening out ballroom dancing, go roller-skating at

# ★★Spice It Up!

## Douse the Handkerchief

Here's a sly plan of action to ensure that your date keeps you in his thoughts for days to come. If your date leaves the table during the course of your dinner date, surreptitiously douse your date's jacket lapel or the handkerchief in his coat pocket with your perfume.

Hours and perhaps days later when he breathes in the fragrance emanating from his handkerchief, not only will he think of you and the wonderful time you had on your date (assuming, of course, the date wasn't a total disaster), but he may also call to ask you out again.

*Note:* This idea works well for guys too. When your date steps away, generously dab some of your cologne onto the lapel of her coat.

the local roller rink, or drive up to Heartbreak Hill and watch the submarine races together.

Whatever you choose to do, make it a special date that your folks will remember fondly. Who knows—in return for such a thoughtful invitation, they may not even impose a curfew!

## "Kidnapping" Date

Before the weekend arrives, draft a "ransom note" with a buddy and mail it to both of your dates, indicating that on a certain day at a specified time, they will have to come up with one million dollars or else they will be "taken captive" for a creative date. Knowing full well who the initiators of this ransom plot are, your dates will wait in anticipation for their "abduction."

When the appropriate time has arrived, knock on your dates' doors, blindfold them, and take them on a wily drive around town to disorient them and disrupt their sense of direction. Once this has been achieved, set out toward your destination, or "hideout."

Once you arrive, help your dates out of the car and walk them down to the water's edge. At this point, remove their blindfolds and unveil the rowboat(s) that will transport you all to the other side of the lake, where a creative picnic lunch awaits your party.

 ## International Cuisine Date

Indulge in a world of culinary pleasures with the International Cuisine Date. Invite your guest couples over for a potluck dinner in which each dish is representative of a particular country. For example, have one person bring Chinese food, another a German dish, and still another Italian fare; other possibilities include Salvadoran, Greek, Mexican, French, and so on. Coordinate with each other who is to bring appetizers, salads, main courses, and desserts to ensure that all courses are covered.

Encourage each couple to come dressed to match the country of their food offering and to bring a selection of music from that land. To enhance everyone's appreciation of the countries represented, have each person read a bit about their country to the group, sharing interesting information about its culture and traditions.

## You Ought to Be in Pictures Date

Going on this date means always knowing where your camera is. With one creative photo after another, the You Ought to Be in Pictures Date can bring more laughs than you may have thought possible.

Hook up with another adventuresome couple and gallivant around town with your camera(s), looking for the most fun, creative, and off-the-wall photo opportunities. Take pictures of each other or even of strangers at the mall, on a college campus, at a sports car lot, and so on. Take photos of interesting or funny billboards and street signs. Let your imaginations run free.

After you have shot several rolls of film, take them to a one-hour photo shop for quick developing. Once the photos are ready, bring them to the place you've chosen for lunch and enjoy each candid snapshot from your creative photo shoot. You may even want to buy photo albums to arrange your photos into a story of the day. Make captions for the pictures or buy the premade captions and thought bubbles at the photo development store.

## Parking Lot Dance Date

Enjoy a great time with friends by spending a midsummer's evening dancing under the stars. Send out invitations to all of your friends and their dates, requesting their presence at this outdoor gala that will begin with a car rally. Ask them to bring snacks and drinks to share.

Once everyone has met at the designated starting location, begin the caravan with a circuitous drive through town until you come upon the vacant parking lot you have chosen for

# ★Spice It Up!

## Write It Down

The next time you find yourself on a double date in a loud and noisy place where having a normal conversation seems nearly impossible, try communicating by writing your thoughts, ideas, and questions on a napkin.

Set some rules in advance, such as no talking. Only a little nudging, smiling, and a fun-loving tickle or two are acceptable. Part of the fun is anticipating your companion's candid and humorous responses, and vice versa, that might not get expressed in a verbal discussion.

Another fun writing exercise for a noisy location is to make up a poem or short story by taking turns writing down one sentence at a time, never knowing where the theme or story will turn next. Or amuse yourselves by drawing funny pictures or playing time-honored games such as tic-tac-toe or hangman. Then take your napkin(s) home as a keepsake of your time together!

the dance. As the drivers pull into the lot, have them park their cars in a big circle facing one another. This will help to form the dance area.

Ask everyone to turn on their parking lights to help illuminate the dance area. (For a strobe effect, have every other car turn on its emergency lights.) Next, have everyone tune in to the same radio station—the one that plays the most popular dance hits—or have someone with a good sound system stand in as DJ for the evening. Create a buffet of party foods by having all the drivers arrange their snacks and drinks on the trunks of their vehicles. Then dance the night away under the stars!

## Catered Dinner Date

An exquisite meal you prepare for friends in your own home has long been one of the most common double-date activities. But the next time you invite your friends over for dinner, make it an evening to impress with the Catered Dinner Date.

Assemble a small crew of servers—friends, roommates, brothers, sisters—who would take pleasure from participating in such a creative event, and have them cater the entire function. Define the duties you would like them to fulfill: Have one be the host or hostess who greets your guests as they arrive and acts as waiter or waitress during dinner. The others can assume the roles of part-time chef (donning a chef's hat and apron, of course) and part-time busboy, respectively.

Your guests will be most impressed with the thought and creativity you put into this special dinner engagement!

## Any Given Sunday Date

One safe way to spend time together on a first date is to invite your date to a function organized by your place of worship. Most places of worship have a full calendar of fun activities going on throughout the week, with something for people at every stage of life, be it high school, college, career single, or married.

Weekend retreats, camping trips, day ski outings, progressive dinners, concerts, day hikes, softball games, and barbecues are just a few of the many events you can expect. This is a great way for both of you to make new friends with other dating couples while being inspired at the same time. If you're really enthusiastic, get involved and volunteer to be on a social committee to help plan the next special event or outing.

## Lucky Lottery Date

Here's a "lottery" you'll want to participate in time and time again. Whereas with traditional lotteries your chances of winning are slim, the Lucky Lottery Date assures you a "rich" time with friends, win or lose.

Begin the evening by having each couple "purchase" a lottery ticket that you've made in advance (for $5, say, or any other agreed-upon amount). That money becomes the lottery jackpot. Next, set a time and dollar limit, such as two hours and $20, and explain to the couples that they have precisely that amount of time to spend that amount of money on a creative date.

When everyone has returned from their evening's activities, have each couple share the details of their creative date. The couple voted by the others as having had the most creative evening receives the Lucky Lottery jackpot. Those who don't win the monetary jackpot still have a jackpot of their own, one filled with fond memories and good times.

## Night Class/Take-a-Lesson Date

Join forces with another couple and sign up at the local community college or adult education center for a one-time class or a low-cost series. Some options to consider are dance classes, automotive repair, woodworking, computer basics, ceramics, photography, and cooking. Find a class

# ⭐Spice It Up!

## Date Kit

Similar to the dating care package, make a crafty box or dating kit and fill it up with goodies, clues, and other hints that will help to unveil the upcoming creative date you have planned. For example, an envelope full of sand could be a clue that you're going to the beach. A plastic box of animal crackers could be a hint that you're going to the zoo. Enjoy the thrill of your date rummaging through your dating kit in an effort to discover additional clues about your date.

To make your dating kit complete, be sure to include some of the following key items: a disposable camera, a postcard of the place you have planned to go, breath mints, and a travel first-aid kit in case your date gives you a fat lip for attempting a kiss on the first date!

that both couples agree on, and develop a new hobby you can do together.

Feel like students again and enjoy planning a study group. Spending so much time together in an academic environment will help you not only learn a new skill but also learn a lot about each other and your pals, while developing an appreciation for the pleasures of participating in activities together.

# CHAPTER 8

# SEASONAL AND SPECIAL-OCCASION DATES

Each year brings a multitude of special occasions that call for celebration—birthdays, graduations, anniversaries, and so on. These times are also ideal for creative dating. After all, what better way to celebrate any occasion than by spending time with someone you care for?

As the seasons change, more fun dating possibilities emerge: a date to celebrate the first snowfall, or an air-conditioned date at the mall when the thermometer hits 100 degrees. The many suggestions for seasonally inspired dates in this chapter will help you recognize the creative dating potential at any time of the year.

 ## Birthday Blast-from-the-Past Date

For a special birthday celebration, take your honey on a mystery adventure through the decades of his or her life. For each decade, do something special that was common to that era. For example, start by driving around and playing music from the '50s, if that's when your date was just a sparkle in his or her parents' eyes. Then go to a '50s diner and share a fountain drink using two straws.

Next, take a drive to the part of town where your sweetie grew up. If that was during the '60s, stop at a park and do some hula-hooping, or head home and tie-dye a shirt. Unveil some childhood photos that you have gathered from one of your date's old albums.

On your next stop, you could visit the high school your date attended in the '70s and bust out the high school yearbook for a hootin' time looking back on the funky styles and poses. Then watch a taped episode of a '70s show or listen to the soundtrack of *Saturday Night Fever*.

Continue the "through the decades" theme leading up to the present time, recognizing significant events in your honey's life that have had special meaning. As a finale, consider arranging a surprise birthday visit or phone call from a childhood friend, teacher, or neighbor—a great way to conclude your journey down memory lane.

## Be My Valentine Date

If there's one day of the year when guys are most susceptible to ending up in the doghouse, it's probably Valentine's Day. It's certainly a day you don't want to put off until the last minute, let alone forget altogether. A quick stop on your way home from work to pick up some roses from a roadside flower stand and a hurried stop to the stationery store to scour through picked-over greeting cards is not exactly a great way to set the romantic tone.

If you're looking to spend more time with your lovely valentine and less time with Fido, consider one or more of the following thoughtful yet affordable ideas to ensure that your next Valentine's Day will be one to make Cupid proud.

* Decorate your valentine's dorm room, office, or bedroom with a barrage of paper hearts, balloons, and crepe-paper streamers.

* Leave a card and a heart-shaped picture frame containing your favorite picture of the two of you, surrounded by rose petals, for your valentine to discover.

* Buy a box of chocolates for your valentine, but remove one or two confections. In their place, leave some heart earrings or a locket to be discovered. Be sure to carefully rewrap the box to avoid the appearance of tampering.

* Make a tape recording of a special Valentine's message that you were inspired to write and sneak it into your honey's cassette player. Leave a note with instructions to press the cassette's play button. At the end of your recorded message, include recordings of love songs that set a romantic mood and have special meaning.

* Fill your valentine's home with red heart-shaped balloons (buy them at a discount from a wholesale party store). Or do the same with flowers from a wholesale outlet.

* Make paper hearts with loving messages on them and leave them in many places for your valentine to discover: car, briefcase, purse, mailbox.

 ## Tax Refund Date

Who would ever think that Uncle Sam would have anything good to offer the world of dating? Tax season is generally perceived not as a special occasion but rather as a cash-flow invasion. You can turn this perception around, however, by making it the theme of a special-occasion date regardless of the outcome.

# ★Spice It Up!

## Candy Valentine Card

Write your sweetheart a romantic note on a sheet of pink or red construction paper. Intermittently throughout your letter, glue down candy hearts that say things like "Be Mine," "I'm Yours," and "True Love" in places where you would otherwise write them in. Leave the card in a special place, accompanied by a vase full of flowers. Upon discovering your surprise, your valentine will be captivated by your creativity and charm.

Part of the fun of this date is to plan an evening working either together or independently (depending on the stage of your relationship) on your tax returns. A pizza, a calculator, and, if you're choosing to complete the long form, a pot of coffee are all the essentials you'll need to make this date add up.

Plan in advance what portion or percentage of your tax refund you wish to dedicate to the date when you celebrate the receipt of your tax refund. Create a "Tax Return Dating Table" that lists the date ideas most suitable for your respective "date brackets." Expect butterflies in your stomach as you draw near your final calculations.

No tax refund due? Although you may be paying Uncle Sam this year (in which case, see chapter 4, "Simple and Free Dates"), there's always next year. If the calculator totals things up in your favor, however, let the planning for your celebration begin (see chapter 10, "Splurge Dates").

## Opening-Day Date

There's a certain thrill and an electrifying feeling you get when you take part in celebrating opening day of an event or season. Arguably, one of the most notable opening days is the start of the professional baseball season, when the boys of summer take the field for the first time of the year. But every month of every season brings other recognizable and not-so-recognizable opening days that can be a hit with you and your date.

Here are a few Opening-Day Date ideas that may help "spring" your dating relationship into action and maybe even cause you to "fall" in love.

### Opening day for ...

- ... hunting and fishing season. (The biggest catch just might be your date.)
- ... a musical or play. (Standing in line for hours for front-row tickets can be part of the fun.)
- ... an amusement or theme park. (They're not just for kids anymore.)
- ... local and regional festivals. (Hit arts-and-crafts fairs, harvest festivals, seasonal bazaars, and so on.)
- ... a new Hollywood film. (Dress up and pretend you're at a celebrity sneak preview.)
- ... a new department store. (There's usually a free gift waiting for the first 100 people who attend the grand opening.)
- ... the school year. (Parents, go celebrate. It's been a long summer!)

Opening-Day Dates are especially great first dates because they represent a new start and are certain to leave a lasting memory.

# U-Pick Date

Have you ever had a hankerin' for Grandma's old-fashioned homemade pies? If so, make a date to replicate that down-home goodness.

To do this date right, get up early and drive out to the local farm or orchard. Depending on the season, you may be able to get apples, strawberries, blackberries, raspberries, cherries, or peaches. Pick a bucket or two of your favorite fruit and bring them home. Together, bake a pie using a recipe that has been handed down in your family or one from your favorite cookbook. Once your pie is done, top it off with some homemade ice cream for a real treat.

If you really enjoy the farm life, pick a bucket of apples, rent a cider press (from the farmer), and make some delicious apple cider. If it's chilly out, you may want to then heat this up on the stove with a few cinnamon sticks. Not only is it delicious and warm, it also makes your home smell wonderful. Other possibilities include making fruit jam, jelly, or cobbler. To really spice things up, mix in a friendly berry fight (no apples), and make the loser do cleanup duty.

# Halloween Date

Invite your date over the day before Halloween. Start your evening by carving pumpkins that you can then put on display for the little ghosts and goblins who will be trick-or-treating at your door the following evening. Have a pumpkin-carving contest with fun categories (scariest, most creative, closest resemblance to your date!). Have a neighbor or roommate(s) be the impartial judge. Come up with your own trick-or-treat prizes to award each other.

Continue the fun by adorning the front porch and living room with Halloween decorations. Create a festive atmosphere that includes a pumpkin patch with straw, cornstalks, a scarecrow, baby pumpkins and gourds, bowls of candy corn, and other homemade decorations. Appeal to the senses by roasting some pumpkin seeds, whose aroma will fill the air, or lighting a spiced pumpkin–scented candle. Have some scary Halloween music in the background (you can borrow it from the local library).

Planning to attend a Halloween costume party? If so, continue your date by teaming up to create your own costumes. Pay a visit to a local consignment store for some inexpensive pieces of clothing, and bring them home for some custom tailoring.

To keep the fun going, visit a haunted house sponsored by one of your local community organizations, and get spooked before returning home to watch a scary movie.

## Pre-Thanksgiving Bash Date

Most people spend Thanksgiving Day with their families, eating until it's not possible to eat any more. If you want to celebrate Thanksgiving with that special someone (without the pressure of family!), consider celebrating a week or two early with your own Pre-Thanksgiving Bash (PTB).

This date takes a little advance planning, but it's part of the fun. Get together to create a menu and shopping list. You can make this a date for just the two of you, or invite some other couples. Once you have all the ingredients and recipes, start the fun of cooking. One person can be in charge of the stuffing, while another takes care of the pie. This can easily turn into an all-day affair. And don't feel restricted to the usual Thanksgiving fare. Create your own traditions!

You can also make decorations for the centerpiece—outline your hand on paper to make a turkey just like you did as a kid or arrange some gourds and pumpkins with fall leaves. Set the table and get ready to indulge in your first annual PTB meal!

 ## Twelve Days of Fitness Date

One sure way to overcome the "battle of the bulging waist" during the winter holidays is a "Twelve Days of Fitness" date. For each "day of fitness," list an activity or set of exercises to be performed together for that day. Write out your activities as lyrics sung to the tune of "The Twelve Days of Christmas." For example:

> Day One: On the first day of fitness, my true love said to me, "Do twenty sit-ups oh so merrily."
> Day Two: On the second day of fitness, my true love said to me, "Do ten good-form push-ups and twenty sit-ups oh so merrily."

As each day goes by, add a new exercise or activity to the previous day's list. On the twelfth day of fitness, you will have completed a dozen consecutive fitness activities with your date. This is a great way to help you keep fit and to enjoy the company of your date during the holidays.

 ## It's Beginning to Look a Lot Like Christmas Date

There's something special about the Christmas season that draws out the best in humanity. It's a time of giving, of making and sharing memories, of helping the less fortunate, of bringing families together, and of celebrating the true meaning of Christmas. It's also a holiday that lends itself to more festive dating ideas than perhaps any other, in part due to the length of the season, which, according to most department stores these days, starts in August!!

A great way to start your Christmas season is to take your date to a local Christmas tree farm to pick out and cut down your own tree. (In addition to being more fun, it's cheaper than buying one from a tree lot.) Most tree farms will have hot chocolate or hot apple cider on hand to keep you warm as you wander through the fields sizing up the grand, noble, and Douglas firs. Once you tag your tree, cut it down and let the farmhands swing by to prep it and strap it onto your vehicle. If you'd rather not cut down a live tree, some tree farms offer "living" Christmas trees that you can replant after the holidays.

Once you've returned home, cut off any extra-long branches, keeping the cut-off sprigs as further decoration (use them in wreaths and the like), and begin the decorating process. Start a new tradition and buy each other an ornament each year that becomes the first item you place on the tree. Continue decorating your tree with colorful lights, bulbs, tinsel, and stringed popcorn; when you're all done, enjoy placing the final star or angel atop the tree.

Next, put another log on the fire, cuddle up on the couch, and admire your efforts while sipping some eggnog and listening to a full carousel of your favorite Christmas CDs. Relax from the hurriedness of the holidays, and take a moment to share with each other all of the things you are thankful for—like mistletoe, for instance.

Here are some additional ideas to consider incorporating into your Christmas-themed date.

* Take a drive through the neighborhoods to admire the houses adorned with Christmas lights. To ensure that you

don't get rushed by cars driving behind you doing the same thing, park your car and stroll along the sidewalk to take in the beautiful lights at a leisurely pace.

* Help get others into the Christmas spirit by joining a group of carolers on a hay-bale ride around town, singing your favorite Christmas carols. Dress warmly.

* Go to the mall, the post office, or another public place that sponsors an "Angel Tree" bearing names and special Christmas gift wishes from children who are less fortunate. Buy and wrap a gift together, and bring it back to the tree for pickup and delivery.

* Make and decorate Christmas cookies together. This entails putting your heads together over the recipe book to select the kind you want to make, going to the store together to shop for ingredients, and then working together to make and decorate the cookies. Once you're done, enjoy eating them while watching a rented Christmas movie and/or deliver them to relatives, neighbors, or mutual friends.

* Make your own Christmas cards and send them to your friends and relatives.

* Put aside the commercialism and hype of the holidays and go to an event that enables you to reflect on the true meaning of Christmas. Attend a Christmas musical, a singing Christmas tree, or a re-enactment of the Christmas story. Read each other the Christmas story beforehand.

## Shortest Day of the Year Date

It happens only once a year—and if you live in the Northern Hemisphere, it's going to happen on December 21. During the winter solstice, daylight lasts for an average of only eight

# ✭Spice It Up!

## Summer Noel

Have you ever received a Christmas card in June? Any occasion can be the right occasion when you want to send a special thank you or greeting to your date, even if it is a little out of season. Inside the Christmas card, you may write something like, "Gee, can you believe it's almost that time of year again?" or "I thought I would beat the Christmas rush by mailing early this year!" Whatever the holiday, a cheerful greeting is always appreciated.

Be sure to thank your date for the fun time you had on your last outing together and suggest doing something again soon. Use your imagination, and remember that a card doesn't necessarily have to be sent on the appropriate holiday!

hours. With so few hours, there's no time to waste. Make the shortness of the day the theme of your date.

To start, make a short call to your date to say you'll be dropping by shortly in your shortbed truck. You'll want to get an early start, so think about fueling up at a breakfast stop and having a short stack of pancakes. Over breakfast, read each other a short article from the morning newspaper before paying the bill. Whatever you do, though, don't be short on your tip, or your waiter or waitress might give you a kick in the shorts on your way out the door.

Next, go to a video store and rent *Get Shorty* or another appropriate title. If it's not as entertaining as you thought, cut it short and do something else (something that's short and sweet, of course). Be quick, but don't rush yourself too much; you don't want to get short of breath. If you do, you'll have to stop and rest, thereby feeling like you're getting the short end of the . . . well, you know.

 ## Create-Your-Own-Holiday Date

Pick a day on the calendar and, together, declare it as your own special holiday. Let the fun begin with a holiday brainstorming session. Since this is your own holiday, you have the freedom to determine its significance, its customs, and, of course, its name. Call it something obvious and meaningful, like "Spill the Beans Day," the day one of you first revealed that you were in love. Or perhaps name it something obscure and secretive, like "Snarfblat Founder's Day," which may have absolutely no relation to the true meaning of your holiday but is sure to keep others guessing when they see it marked on your calendar.

Treat this day just as you would a real holiday, and take time off from work to celebrate it. Have a blast drumming up creative ideas and customs certain to make the day one worth anticipating. It can be something as simple as mailing each other a romantic letter that includes a surprise or having your pictures taken together each year at the exact same place in the exact same pose. Or make it lavish, such as toasting each other while being serenaded on a moonlit gondola ride through romantic waterways or taking a hot-air balloon ride over the countryside. You can even make it adventurous and go skydiving. Try giving each other a kiss during a free-fall!

Be sure to detail such important things as what "traditional" foods, colors, music, dress, guests (if any), and so on will be represented as part of this undeclared national holiday. These details will help your holiday rival all others.

 ## A Date for All Seasons

Whether it's spring, summer, winter, or fall, each season brings with it one certainty—change. But change is good. It encourages variety, and we all know that variety is the spice of life. The same can be said for your dating life! With each change of season comes many new opportunities for excitement, renewal, and diversity in your dating experience.

Although it may be true, depending on where you live, that certain seasons may appear to show favor over others, there still remains the fact that dating is for all seasons. Here are several "seasonal" date ideas to consider throughout the year to avoid having your dating life go into hibernation.

### Winter

* Make a date to celebrate the first snowfall.
* Go to the mountains for some four-wheeling. Once you arrive, make a snowman.
* Go cross-country skiing through the wilderness. Camp out in a yurt.
* Spend a day on the slopes snowboarding or downhill skiing.
* Rent snowmobiles for the afternoon and carve it up in the meadows.
* Bundle up and go for a daring walk in subzero temperatures, with hot chocolate to follow.
* Help each other fulfill a healthful New Year's resolution—exercising, eating right, or taking Geritol twice a day. Have an inaugural date to kick off your resolution, and plan a celebration once you achieve your goal.
* Celebrate Groundhog Day. (Why not? Bill Murray thought it was something worth repeating again and again.)

### Spring

* Create a May basket together. Pick some flowers, arrange them in a basket, and leave it anonymously on a neighbor's doorstep.
* Visit a rose garden or a Japanese garden and have a picnic.
* Strap on the rain gear and go puddle jumping in the rain.
* Celebrate the time change. Plan something fun around the extra hour in the day.
* Plant a garden with a variety of your favorite flowers or vegetables.
* Pack a pair of rods and reels and go on a fishing expedition.
* Put on your grubbies and do spring cleaning around the house. Have a garage sale the next weekend.

### Summer

* Kick off the summer with a barbecue.
* Go to the county or state fair, have fun on the rides, eat cotton candy, and win your date a stuffed animal.
* Go on a relaxing float trip down a river on a raft. If you're feeling adventuresome, make it a white-water rafting trip.
* Celebrate the longest day of the year (summer solstice). Start at dusk and end at dawn.
* Go on a nature hike and take a rest stop at a waterfall.
* Go on an air-conditioned date at the mall when the thermometer hits 100 degrees.

### Fall

* Celebrate your last day of freedom before starting back to school.
* Attend the first football game of the fall season (high school, college, or professional).
* Take a drive in the country to witness the autumn leaves changing colors.

* Celebrate Oktoberfest.
* Rake a pile of leaves as high as you can and jump in them for old times' sake.
* Get up early on the weekend, throw on a hat and warm sweats, and meet at a hole-in-the-wall restaurant for a great breakfast.
* Stay indoors during the inclement weather. Kick back and relax together by reading a book.

Each season brings unique dating possibilities. Find an activity as unique as you and your date to make each season a special occasion.

# CHAPTER 9

# WACKY AND WHIMSICAL DATES

Iff you consider yourself adventuresome and a little on the spunky side, you're going to get a wallop out of the ideas this chapter has to offer. Even if you consider yourself a conservative dater, you just might find yourself attempting a few of these zany ideas. They're sure to make your next date a real escapade!

For many off-the-wall date ideas, like the Rooftop Rendezvous Date, Island Divider, or the Topsy-Turvy Date, you need to look no further than this chapter. Once you catch the bizarre dating bug, you'll be well on your way to creating your own quaint and quirky ideas for dates destined to make the Wacky and Whimsical Dating Hall of Fame.

 ## Whale-Watching Extravaganza Date

Now here's a crafty date that even Moby Dick would be certain to "spout" home about. On a nice sunny day, ask your date to join you for a whale-watching adventure. This date, however, is not your ordinary whale-watching excursion.

Prior to the actual date, promote this special day by telling your sweetheart about how whales migrate seasonally and how they can often be seen close to shore when they feed. Let your date know that rather than taking a chartered boat ride, the two of you will be having a picnic on the jetty, where you will be able to spot the whales through binoculars. (A novice whale watcher will find this credible.)

Now for the unexpected: On your way to the jetty, park your car near one of the marina's parking lots. Your date will become curious when you spread out a blanket for a picnic on a plot of well-manicured grass—an unusual place to stop since you are still a good several hundred yards from the jetty.

Soon, though, your date will figure out what you have up your sleeve, because directly across the street from you will be a famous Wylan whale mural, skillfully painted on the facade of a large building. (Wylan's murals can be found in many cities up and down the western and eastern seaboards.) If your area has no whale murals, picnic outside a store that displays whale sculptures in its window or near photos of whales that you set up. At that moment, your date will realize that you have purposely arranged for this date to be a make-believe whale-watching extravaganza.

Sit down, enjoy your picnic, and take turns looking through your binoculars, pretending that you're truly on a sightseeing tour. Be entertained by the inquisitive stares of people walking, jogging, or skating near this unusual setting for a picnic.

Only a picture could serve as proof of this "whale of a tale" that you both will later delight in recounting to your family and friends. (Note: You may want to include in your date's lunch a coupon good for a real whale-watching extravaganza in the future!)

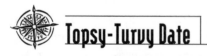 ## Topsy-Turvy Date

If the dating game sometimes seems to go in the wrong direction for you, don't resist it. Instead, celebrate it by making

# ✯Spice It Up!

## Dating Arrivals

It's time once again to pick up your date. As generally expected, you arrive at your date's house by car. Routine and predictable. So maybe it's time to try adding a new twist to picking up your date—something a little out of the ordinary.

The next time you arrive at your date's door, do it in a creative style. You might show up on rollerskates, for example. Bring a pair for your date to put on, and then skate off together to your car, which is parked several blocks away. What a unique way to start your evening together. Here are some other out-of-the-ordinary modes of transportation to consider when picking up your date: tandem bicycle, moped, golf cart, horse, limousine, go-cart, piggy-back!

your next date a real topsy-turvy event. Even if you're on top of your dating game, it's good to shake things up a little now and then by breaking out of the conventional dating pattern in favor of an upside-down, inside-out, or reverse approach.

To make this date a successful flop (!), consider one or more of the following off-the-wall ideas:

* Planning on dinner and a movie? Reverse the order and see the movie first. This way you get the matinee prices, and you don't have to spend a fortune on soda and popcorn because you'll be having a meal soon.

* Surprise your date with dinner (rather than breakfast) in bed. You may want to serve something that's gentle on the stomach, like pepperoni pizza and Pepto-Bismol, or tacos and Tums.

* Invite your date over for a romantic candlelight dinner—of bacon, eggs, and pancakes.
* Spoil your appetites with dessert and coffee first, and then share an entrée. Finish with an appetizer.
* Order clam chowder in a sourdough bowl and start eating the bowl first (well, at least until it starts to flow over the sides!).
* At the beginning of your date, greet your sweetheart with "Good night" and a kiss before walking him or her to your car.
* Switch roles and have the woman pick up the man. Gals, enjoy mustering up the courage to ask your man out and then plan for a future date. Open the doors for him and order the meal (pay the bill, too!). Guys, feel what it's like to scramble to be dressed and ready on time before your date picks you up, or be patient with your date when she seems lost but is determined to get you to your destination without consulting a map.

No matter what you choose to do, mix it up in some way to show your fun and creative side.

 ## Brown-Bagger Surprise Date

If your date has a good sense of humor and an appreciation of the unexpected, you may be ideal candidates for the not-so-predictable Brown-Bagger Surprise Date.

Invite your date to have lunch with you at an exquisite restaurant. Once you arrive at the restaurant's parking lot, escort your date toward the trunk of your car. Stop, pop open the trunk, pull out two folding chairs and a couple of brown-bag lunches from the cooler (prepared earlier by you), and have a creative lunch together on the restaurant property. Remember, you invited your date to have lunch *at* the restaurant, not *in* the restaurant! Be brave and have your lunch right there in the parking lot as if you were having a tailgater, or relocate under a shady tree nearby.

No matter what location you choose for your Brown-Bagger Date, be sure to make your time together fun for all to see. To ensure your date's faith in future lunch engagements with you, be sure to include in your date's lunch a promissory note or coupon good for a future lunch *inside* the restaurant.

## Half a Date

Is your schedule packed? Are work pressures keeping you from having fun? Does there seem to be no time for dating? If time isn't on your side, no need to worry. Don't let the lack of time hinder your dating life. It's okay to have an "express" date once in a while (such as meeting for coffee or a walk in the park), especially if your only other option is to not have a date at all.

Here's a creative idea to consider, however, that's a little off center from your typical abbreviated date. The idea of the Half a Date is to participate in as many aspects of a regular date as possible, but in half the time.

Start by meeting your date at half past the hour, at a location that's the halfway point between your homes. Once you meet, take one car approximately halfway to your destination—a basketball game, for instance—and stop for a quick bite to eat. Halfway through your meal, switch plates and eat half of the other person's dinner. Or don't switch at all and stay with your own meal if you requested half an order. Celebrating a belated birthday? Order a piece of cake to split in half, and blow out half a candle.

While at the basketball game, go to the concession stand at halftime and share a rope of red licorice—half for your date and half for you. Start at either end of the rope, meeting halfway for a kiss! (Full or half—it's up to you.)

Continue the Half a Date theme by walking your date halfway back to the car; then stop and indulge in half a hug and half a kiss, or plant kisses all over half of your date's face, before calling it a night.

## Candlelight Fast-Food Dinner Date

Call it crazy, a little esoteric, and maybe borderline offbeat, but when was the last time you went to a fast-food restaurant and shared a romantic candlelight dinner for two over a couple of kiddie meals?

Find a corner table, cover it with a nice tablecloth, and place a candle in the middle as a centerpiece. Bring two wine glasses, and fill them with your favorite soft drink. Bring silverware and cloth napkins for an extra touch of class. If you dare, arrange for a limousine to provide transportation to and from the distinguished establishment. Following dinner, entertain yourselves with a merry time in the children's playground.

## Rooftop Rendezvous Date

It's said that location is everything. Most people would agree that it can make or break a business, for example. With the Rooftop Rendezvous Date, a nicely elevated location with an interesting view is the most important element of all. (Two folding chairs and a picnic lunch are secondary elements.)

Here's one example of the Rooftop Rendezvous Date: If you're on a college campus, have the date in a place where you can recline in two folding chairs overlooking the campus and watch the multitude of students scampering off to

# ★★★ Spice It Up!

## Singing Telegram

For a bang of a start to any date or special occasion, arrive at your date's door with the gift of a singing telegram. Whether it is sung by you or by hired talent (friend or professional), be sure to capture every moment of this serenading spectacle on film. Sing a song that you wrote yourself, or sing a funny jingle that describes the date you're about to go on.

If the hired talent exceeds your budget, be creative and bring along a portable stereo or boom box, and lip-sync a recorded love song from an opera star. Go all out by wearing a tux with tails (borrowed to keep the cost down) and, of course, come with a flower or balloon bouquet to be handed to your date from this evening's Prince Charming.

class. Meanwhile, you and your date can contemplate the merits of attending class versus enjoying a creative lunch date and people-watching.

Other lofty locations for the Rooftop Rendezvous include a housetop, the roof of a carport, a grandstand, a tree fort, a bridge . . . or even the Empire State Building! *Note:* Before attempting this date, make sure your date isn't afraid of heights!

 ## Sidewalk Cafe Date

When it comes to dining atmosphere, a charming cafe with outdoor seating ranks high among restaurantgoers. But it pales in comparison with the atmosphere created by the crazy Sidewalk Cafe Date.

. What sets this date apart from any ordinary lunch date is that the Sidewalk Cafe Date's location is truly on a sidewalk—outside your own residence! Your date will be surprised when he or she realizes that you have carefully organized your own outdoor cafe, one that embodies nearly all the features of a real cafe, including a table set for two, a menu, a food cart, a coat rack, a table centerpiece, and after-dinner mints.

Post a placard nearby reading "Welcome to the Sidewalk Cafe," so there will be no mistaking the aim of this obscure engagement. Arrange to have a roommate, family member, or friend act as your waiter for the day, by serving you a delicious meal that you and your friends have prepared in advance. Don't forget to leave a tip!

 **Just Married Date**

If you and your date are not intimidated by the "M" word, here's a date that will surely be worthy of a good premarital chuckle.

Decorate your car as you would if you had just been married. Tie balloons, streamers, and tin cans to the rear bumper and write the words "Just Married" all over the windows. Drive around town honking your horn and watching the reactions of the onlookers as they delight in your faux marriage celebration.

On the same day, visit a jewelry store and try on engagement rings, just as if you're only months away from tying the knot. See how convincing you can be as you role-play with the jeweler. Think of this date as good practice for the future!

## Laundromat Date

Spending several hours at the laundromat doesn't rank high on most people's fun-to-do list. But inviting your date to do laundry with you can make washing clothes a much more interesting event. Pack a lunch or some snacks, and get ready to learn a little something more about each other while your laundry washes and dries!

Start by sharing your personal washing methods, routines, and quirks. Enlighten each other by comparing laundry soaps and fabric softeners. Waiting for the cycle to finish is the perfect time to learn more about each other.

If you're feeling a little crazy, give each other rides in the laundry carts. Then toss the clothes in the dryer and treat your date to a soda from the vending machine. Prepare for the Laundromat Date's finale: the Big Fold. Have a contest to see who can fold the fastest or the neatest!

## Pizza Date

Ever wonder how you can make a delicious pizza taste even better? Try sprinkling on some creativity to see just how much "flavor" you can add to this already great-tasting meal.

Order a pizza to go and take it to an unusual location to share with your date, such as the gazebo in the park, the fifty-yard line of a football field, or the tailgate of your pickup truck (parked at a viewpoint overlooking the city). Select a location that has special significance to both of you.

If you want to add an element of surprise to this date, arrange in advance to have the pizza delivered to the creative location where you and your date will be: near the water fountain at the mall, on a park bench while feeding the squirrels, or up in a tree fort, for instance. Tip the delivery person well, and be sure to give excellent directions when you order, so that you avoid a no-show. (If you're perched in a tree fort and have to stall until a belated pizza arrives, it could be a long and awkward wait.)

 ## Drive-In Movie Date

We all know what type of reputation a date at the drive-in movies can have. We also know the reservations parents can have when their daughter is asked out to a double feature. Here's an idea that will win Mom and Dad's approval and will likely get them involved in setting it up.

Invite your date to the drive-in movies. On your way to the drive-in, pretend that you forgot your wallet at her parents' house and must return to get it. Once back home, pull into the driveway and push the button of the garage door opener. As the door slowly opens, your date will be startled to see a big-screen TV, a VCR, and several large movie posters (picked up earlier by you at the video rental store) tacked on the walls.

As the previews begin, your date's dad will enter from the side garage door, holding a squirt bottle in one hand and a squeegee in the other, and proceed to clean the windshield to assure good visibility. A tap on the horn will bring Mom out with a batch of homemade popcorn and some sodas to enjoy as you sit back and take in a cozy movie night at the homestead.

## A Date at the Office

When it comes to work, the word "date" usually brings to mind matters related to appointments, business meetings, and deadlines. But you can change that perception when you schedule a creative date at the office!

Check your work schedules and confirm a meeting to have lunch together during the week at your date's place of work. Then surprise your date with a creative picnic lunch: Pack a picnic basket full of goodies, a blanket to spread out on the floor, and a couple of seat cushions. To add a classy touch, borrow a vase of flowers from the receptionist's desk and place it in the middle of your blanket.

To help facilitate this date, have several of your date's coworkers (including the boss, if possible) participate in helping to set it up. Appointments like these can make work something to look forward to!

## Island Divider Dinner Date

A formal dinner date on a boulevard's median strip is arguably one of the most outlandish date ideas ever. But to the crazy dater, nothing's out of the question! You may not want to choose this date if you live in a big city where island dividers are littered and noisy. But if you live in a smaller city or town, this could be one of the more unique dates you go on!

For this adventure, dress up in formal garb and have a cheerful dinner catered by friends on a safe, grassy island divider. A quiet table for two is simply out of the question for this public dating spectacle. Anticipate a continual flow of honking horns from passing drivers admiring your dating prowess.

# ★★Spice It Up!

## Chocolate Kiss

Does your stomach turn cartwheels at the thought of being turned down for a kiss? If so, here's an idea that might save you from feeling embarrassed or rejected if this should happen, and "sweeten" your dating experience at the same time.

The next time you'd like to kiss your date, be sure to have a handful of chocolate candy kisses in your pocket. (If it's a hot day, you may want to find another way to carry your candy kisses. Otherwise it could be a very sticky situation!) Ask your date if you may give him or her a kiss. If the answer is yes, then by all means, kiss! If you get turned down, however, casually pull a handful of the chocolates from your pocket and say, "Are you sure? You don't know what you're missing!" You will have avoided a potentially uncomfortable situation with a "tasteful" use of humor.

## Progressive Fast-Food Dinner Date

Here's an idea that will add some "flavor" to your next four-course meal: Invite your date to a progressive dinner.

Begin with an appetizer at a fast-food Mexican place. An order of nachos would be an excellent choice. Next, drive to a burger place for a luscious dinner salad. For your main course, spare no expense with a trip to another fast-food eatery for your favorite combo meal. Conclude your four-course extravaganza with a frosty dessert at the nearest ice cream shop. (You may also want to stop at a local pharmacy afterward for some antacid!)

## "Mission Impossible" Date

Send your date a package marked "TOP SECRET," containing a cassette tape with a recorded message on it. The message will convey to your date your instructions as to the upcoming "mission" you have strategically planned for the two of you. Include in the message "classified" information, including the time and place you plan to meet, the appropriate attire for the occasion, and any other significant clues that will set your date to speculating about what this clandestine adventure might be.

Be sure to conclude the tape with these famous words: "Your mission, should you choose to accept it, is to have the most wonderful time possible on your date. This tape will self-destruct in five seconds."

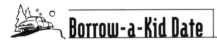

## Borrow-a-Kid Date

Have you ever wondered what it would feel like to be a kid again? Are you a "kid at heart"? Does the child within you desire to come out every now and then? If so, here's the opportunity you've been waiting for. Bring back the days of your youth, while enjoying a date with a compelling grown-up. Who could ask for more?

On your next date, invite your little brother or sister, a nephew or niece, or the next-door neighbor's kid to spend the day with the two of you. Whoever you and your date decide to "borrow," make that child the center of attention throughout your entire time together.

Go to the carnival or county fair. Take the child on the kiddie rides, and be sure to visit the petting zoo. Perhaps spend an afternoon in the park playing on the swings and the merry-go-round. Pack a lunch fit for a kid that includes all your childhood favorites: peanut butter and jelly sandwiches, animal crackers, fruit juice, and so on.

After a full day of activities, return home and watch an animated movie or take a nap, whichever seems most inviting. Afterward, play a few classic board games such as Candyland or Chutes and Ladders to cap off a date fit for kids of all ages.

 ## Par for the Course Date

One hour before sunset, take your date to a fluffy sand trap along a secluded putting green at a nearby golf course. Be sure to get the consent of the golf course management first, of course! Spread out a blanket in the bunker and enjoy a mid-evening picnic on the sandy shores of the fifteenth green, or whichever one offers the most scenic view.

To add to the ambiance, bring along a CD or tape player and have some music playing in the background. After your picnic, break out a couple of putters and some golf balls so you can putt for kisses on the green as the sun goes down. Don't rule out bringing some glow-in-the-dark golf balls or a camping lantern so you can try your hands at a little night putting!

# CHAPTER 10

# SPLURGE DATES

N ot every date is destined to be a discount date. Every dating relationship has times when it's appropriate to spend extravagantly. Maybe you're celebrating a special occasion, maybe it's your anniversary, or maybe you just won the lottery. Whatever the case, if you're ready to impress, go on a spree, spend lavishly, indulge, go all out, throw money around, or go hog wild, then read on. In this chapter, you will find many date ideas that will make your splurging fun, exciting, and worth every penny.

## Train Ride Date

Here's a fun date to engineer. Choose a splendid afternoon to invite your date out to lunch. Tell your date that you need to stop by the train station first to pick up an important package you've been eagerly awaiting. As you both enter the depot, surprise your date with two prepaid train tickets to a nearby city, where you have planned a full day of fun!

Once you have arrived at your destination, rent bicycles for the afternoon and tour the city, exploring gift shops, neighborhoods, and parks. Comb the entertainment section of the local newspaper for a jazz concert or an art festival on the waterfront. Before the trip home, enjoy a relaxing

# ★★★ Spice It Up!

## The Envelope, Please

Put on your thinking cap and come up with three great ideas for an upcoming creative date with that someone special. Make a coupon for each date idea, and then seal each one separately in an envelope. On the outside of each envelope write "Date 1," "Date 2," and "Date 3," respectively.

Instruct your date to choose one of the three envelopes to discover the theme of your creative date for the evening. Will it be the Dinner Theater Date? The Harbor Cruise Dinner Date? Or the Take Me Out to the Ballgame Date? "The envelope, please . . ." Enjoy the suspense as your date unveils your activity for the evening.

If your date curiously asks about the activities sealed in the other envelopes, simply say, "We'll have to go out again for you to find out what they are." What a clever ploy to encourage a second and third date!

dinner at a quaint restaurant where you've made reservations in advance.

Oh, and about that package you needed to pick up? Once you return to the train station where you began, do the railroad shuffle over to the baggage counter to pick up the parcel—which, coincidentally, will be addressed not to you but to your date! What a surprise it will be when your date opens the package and finds a collection of mementos from the day you've just spent together (such as a book of matches from the restaurant where you dined, a postcard from the museum you visited, or a T-shirt from the university campus you rode your bikes through).

Your date will be impressed by your thoughtfulness when you acknowledge modestly that you picked up these items on the previous weekend, when you went to the city to scout out your activity plan for this date. What a great way to get your dating relationship on track—or "back" on track, as the case may be!

## Cultural Date

Every couple deserves a little culture in their lives. And what better way to experience it than through the avenue of dating? Begin by having dinner at a foreign restaurant with authentic decor, where you can enjoy the tastes and sensations of another country. Following dinner, experience the cultural arts by visiting an art gallery or a museum. If you prefer the performing arts, consider attending an opera, ballet, or symphony. A Broadway show would be a terrific option as well. Whichever you decide, you'll be assured a cultural experience, although for the novice it may be more of a cultural shock!

## Carriage Ride Date

Revisit the gracious era of the horse and buggy with an after-dinner carriage ride. Cuddle up in the coach, sip some hot chocolate, and enjoy a regal, chauffeur-guided tour through town. Make it a surprise by keeping your date unaware of your plan until it's time to board.

A horse-drawn carriage is a wonderful setting in which to present your date with a special gift appropriate for the occasion (birthday, anniversary, engagement, special holiday) or to simply whisper sweet nothings to one another.

## Dinner Cruise Date

For an experience your date will never forget, hop aboard a yacht that offers a sumptuous champagne brunch or an elegant dinner cruise through the harbor's waterways. Whichever you choose, you'll be assured three to four hours of sailing fun. Dress up and make it a formal affair.

After enjoying the pleasures of dining maritime style, take a walk along the deck and enjoy the panoramic views the city has to offer as your captain navigates your yacht along the waterfront. Dance to the lively music. Sail into the sunset.

If you live in an area far from a harbor or bay, consider a river cruise on a sternwheeler or steamboat. If it's a cool night, give your jacket to your date and be a hero!

## Dinner for Two with Roses for You Date

What could be more romantic than a candlelight dinner for two at a lavish restaurant boasting an unrivaled bill of fare and atmosphere? This type of date is popular among couples celebrating an anniversary, birthday, Valentine's Day, or simply a "Just Because You're Special Day."

To commemorate your next special affair, try adding an additional bit of extravagance to your evening's agenda. Select a restaurant that suits both of your preferences, and then make arrangements with the maitre d' to reserve a private table for two. In advance of your date, leave an elegant arrangement of roses with the staff, which they will place on your private table before you return.

When the two of you arrive at the restaurant, watch for the surprised look on your date's face when you are escorted to the table adorned with the beautiful floral centerpiece you've provided. A thoughtful touch like this will be remembered for a long time.

 ## Your Lucky Day Date

A great way to avoid the trap of redundant and predictable dating is to add a little flair (financial or otherwise) to a would-be ordinary date. Two hours before you pick up your date, go to each establishment where you will be taking your date (restaurant, ice cream parlor, movie theater, and so on) and pay for everything in advance. As the evening unfolds, enjoy the surprised look on your date's face when, time after time, the two of you become the recipients of "free" dinners, "free" ice cream, "free" movie admission, and so on.

Have an employee from each establishment participate by greeting the two of you with "good news," such as "Congratulations, this is your lucky day! You have just won a free dinner!" or "Congratulations, you are our 100th customer today and are entitled to free ice cream!" or perhaps "Congratulations! Tonight is couples' night, and you're the lucky couple chosen to win free passes to a movie of your choice!"

 ## Chauffeured Dinner and Movie Date

Since the advent of the silver screen, going out for dinner and a movie has arguably become one of the most common dates

# ⋆⋆ Spice It Up!

## Dating Coupon Booklet

Think of as many fun and frugal activities as you can that you and your special someone would enjoy doing together when out on a date. Once you have come up with a multitude of ideas, make a coupon for each activity and bundle them into a coupon booklet. Present the booklet to your date the next time you're together. Be sure to include on each coupon any relevant information, such as expiration date, coupon value (good for…), and any other important details essential for each date to transpire. Encourage your date to redeem them frequently.

Here are several creative ways you can choose to organize and/or present your creative dating coupon booklet:

**Monthly Dating Madness Coupon Booklet:** Come up with 12 terrific dating activities, one for each month of the year. These activities would be those that require some advance planning and are best scheduled ahead of time (i.e., concert, hot-air balloon ride, water skiing).

**Random Dating Rendezvous Coupon Booklet:** Include coupons for a creative mix of fun and affordable activities that can be redeemed "at random." Coupons might include picking out a recipe from a magazine or cookbook so you can prepare a meal together or hitting a garage sale early and picking out a piece of old furniture so you can restore it together.

**Create-a-Date Coupon Booklet:** Assemble a creative dating coupon booklet exclusively for use on one particular date. Using a menu approach, encourage your date to choose one of two coupon options for each component of your date (i.e., dinner, entertainment, dessert, etc.). If your first activity of the evening is dining, your date will have two dining options to choose from. Continue with this format for each segment of your date. (See "Creative Dating Coupons" for more ideas.)

around. Although it is often enjoyable, it can also become rather bland. The Chauffeured Dinner and Movie Date, however, demonstrates how you can turn the ordinary dinner-and-a-movie date into something more memorable!

Instead of the typical car arrival and pickup, this date begins with a stately limousine entrance followed by a luxurious ride to dinner—a classy way to make your date feel special. But this regal beginning is only a prelude to what's to come. Your date will feel like a royal dignitary from start to finish.

When the limousine arrives to pick up your date, a small red carpet that you have brought along is rolled out from the limousine door by the waiting chauffeur. In the limo, enjoy an appetizer of wine and cheese en route to the restaurant. Upon entering the restaurant, the maitre d' (whom you have spoken with earlier in the day and pretipped generously) immediately turns his attention to his "honored guests" and leads you to the establishment's finest table, which is brimming with romantic ambiance.

Following a scrumptious dinner, return to your limousine and proceed to a local theater, where you have made plans to see a movie on its opening night. Awaiting your arrival are two of your buddies, dressed up like security guards or Secret Service agents. Have them provide you and your date with a VIP escort to the theater doors.

After the movie, enjoy a splendid drive through the big city. At the appointed time, your chauffeur pulls over and parks, as if to allow you and your date to enjoy the cityscape. What your date doesn't know, however, is that the limo is parked directly beneath a pedestrian bridge or skywalk. Moments later, your date gets a surprise visit from a teddy bear on a string that is lowered into the opened moonroof by a friend overhead. The teddy bear is holding a red rose and a card that says "I Love You" or "You're Special" or any other appropriate message. (How about "Will You Marry Me?")

This is a great date to consider if you hope to leave a lasting impression.

##  Dot-Com Date

You don't have to be an Internet geek to enjoy the benefits of a high-tech date. The activities involved in the Dot-Com Date are the same whether you're online or off; it's the planning process that makes this date one for the information age.

Take advantage of the Internet's seemingly unlimited information and resources to make your next date a real start-up! Below are some of the many possibilities. (Opentable.com and Citysearch.com offer their services only in selected cities, but you can use the other sites no matter where you live.)

* Buy flowers for your date from Flowers.com.
* Make dinner reservations via Opentable.com.
* Select a recipe from Recipes.com, have groceries and a movie brought to your door, and order a bottle of wine from Wine.com.
* Visit Citysearch.com to learn about activities and events in your city.
* Rent a DVD movie from Netflix.com.
* Play a game on Flipside.com.

Your date will be impressed with your high-tech know-how. Whoever would have thought the Internet could be such an asset when it comes to dating!

# ★★Spice It Up!

## A Surprise Wherever You Go

Do you want to dazzle your date? Leave a lasting impression? Demonstrate your creativity? One way to accomplish all this and more is to plan to have a string of gifts given and discovered throughout the course of your date.

For example, as you're walking through the mall, a worker from the flower cart suddenly calls out, "Carolina (or whatever your date's name is), these flowers are for you!" Then, when you both pause to look in a shoe-store window, next to a pair of shoes your date has been wanting is a sign reading "Carolina, I'm yours!" Or perhaps you're in a music store listening to new releases when an employee offers to give your date his or her CD of choice for free. Later, when you're sitting down to dinner, your date is surprised to receive a visit from a violinist playing a few romantic melodies.

 **This Is Your Life Date**

Not every date turns out to be what you expected it to be. Creative dating is most fun and effective when it incorporates the element of surprise. Keeping your date on the edge of his or her seat seems to be a common motif among the most creative dates shared in this book. After all, who doesn't like to be surprised? A pinch of creativity here and a smidgen of suspense there are all the ingredients you need to make your next date of Oscar-winning caliber.

Invite your date to a movie "matinee." What your date won't know is that you have reserved the theater at a pre-matinee time and arranged to show a very personal movie: one that tells the story of your date's life via a compilation of home-movie clips and other images that you have assembled and produced. (You may be able to use the audio-video center at a local school or university.)

When you prepare the compilation, include images of your date's childhood, still photos of your date in junior high wearing braces, and so on, right up to the most current images that you can find. Intermittently, include text or a voiceover that helps to tell your date's life story. Include a few minutes of clips from interviews with several of your

# ★★Spice It Up!

## Balloon Bouquet

Personally deliver to your date's workplace a bouquet of balloons in a variety of colors, shapes, and sizes that distinguish the special occasion you intend to celebrate. Get an officemate to help you divert your date's attention as you stealthily tiptoe in for a quick time of decorating and setup. If the office environment is not an option, locate your date's car in the employee parking lot and tie the balloon bouquet onto the car's side mirror or bumper just minutes before your date gets off work. To add even more of a special touch, place little love notes in each balloon prior to blowing them up. Days later, when the balloons eventually deflate, your hidden message can be retrieved, unless of course your date's impatience and a stickpin get to them first!

date's friends, in which they say something special about your date and your relationship, reminisce about memorable moments from childhood, and so on.

For an even greater effect, consider holding this date at a drive-in. It can be a natural lead-in for a marriage proposal. At the end of the movie, go to a restaurant for dinner, where your date's family and friends will be waiting to celebrate this occasion with the two of you.

 **Ice Follies Date**

For a rousing one-of-a-kind adventure suitable for all ages, take your date (and your nephew or niece too, if you'd like) to an Ice Follies spectacular. Revisit your childhood as cartoon themes are brought to life on the ice by world-class figure skaters in extravagant costumes.

During intermission, surprise your date with a box of animal crackers, inside which is a dating coupon (for a future creative date) that you secretly slipped in earlier. Before you leave, be sure to get in line for a souvenir photo with your date that includes the main cartoon characters in the background.

As your Ice Follies Date appears to be drawing to a close, present your date with another surprise: a detour to a local ice-skating rink. Have a splendid time together imitating the show-stopping moves from the production you've just enjoyed. Be supportive of each other, especially if one or both of you are novices, and teach each other how to skate backward. Part of the fun is holding hands as you skate around the rink to avoid creating a few ice "fallies" of your own. Once you're off the ice, conclude the date with some hot chocolate and great conversation until your red noses return to their normal color.

## Home Improvement Date

Whether you view your dating relationship as one under construction and in need of repair, or perhaps one that's new and still at the drawing table, this date is for you. Working on a home improvement project together can be a great relationship builder that promotes teamwork, problem solving, and communication—and also provides a certain degree of comic relief. So consider spending a date together getting grease under your nails and dirt on your face.

Part of the fun of this date is doing the research: Have some microwave popcorn while watching a video on how to fix a leaky faucet or build a tool organizer for your garage! Go to the library together to find a book on how to build a box for an herb garden or a flowerbed. Attend a workshop (offered free at most home improvement warehouses) to learn from the experts how to tile kitchen counters or wallpaper a room.

Once you've identified your project and researched together how best to get the job done, strap on your tool belts and get busy. Keep in mind that not every project needs to be of major proportions. Your Home Improvement Date could be as basic as rearranging the furniture, replacing a showerhead, or painting the walls of a room. To keep with the construction theme, pack a lunch pail full of goodies and have a picnic lunch together near the site of your project.

# CREATIVE DATING COUPONS

reative dating coupons are a great way to initiate a date while minimizing the nervousness that can arise when asking someone out for the first time. Even if you're currently in a relationship, presenting a coupon for a fun, creative date activity is a good way to guarantee that you'll get to spend time with your sweetheart.

From the dating coupon good for a Sentimental Flashback, on which you step back in time to recapture every moment of your very first date, to the one for a $100 Date, on which you spontaneously find fun ways to spend every last penny of a $100 bill, these coupons will help you perpetuate the creative dating experience. Also included are coupons for thoughtful gestures for those occasions when you want to do something special for your sweetheart, such as breakfast in bed or a bouquet of hand-picked flowers.

The best coupons, however, are the ones you create yourself. You can score some serious points with the homemade touch. Be sure to include all the relevant information, such as expiration date, coupon value, and any other important details essential for the date to transpire.

Included in this chapter are many "date-ready" coupons to help you get started, followed by a few "create-your-own." No matter how many you decide to incorporate into your dating routine, you're guaranteed a time of fun and romance. Let the dating begin!

# Dating Coupon

This coupon entitles you to a Splurge Date because you deserve it. Besides, payday is just around the corner!

# Dating Coupon

This coupon entitles you to list your top twelve date ideas, place them in a jar, and pick one each month that we'll do together, starting this month.

# Dating Coupon

This coupon entitles you to be swept away for a "cuddle-up" weekend getaway at a surprise destination.

# Dating Coupon

This coupon recognizes that you've had a tough week and entitles you to be spoiled with a one-hour back or foot rub (or both).

**Dating Coupon**

DOUBLE DATE

# Dating Coupon

This coupon entitles you to go on a double date. You choose the activity and the couple you'd like to share it with.

---

**Dating Coupon**

RAINY DAY

# Dating Coupon

This coupon is good for the purchase of your favorite classic movie on video or DVD and a night at home together watching it. Popcorn included.

---

**Dating Coupon**

THOUGHTFUL

# Dating Coupon

This coupon is good for a bouquet of handpicked flowers (with vase), to be personally delivered to you at home, work, or anywhere . . . you choose.

---

**Dating Coupon**

THOUGHTFUL

# Dating Coupon

This coupon entitles you to your own "fix-it" man (me) for an afternoon of plumbing, painting, repairing, or completing an unfinished project at your home.

**Dating Coupon**

FUN AND FRUGAL

# Dating Coupon

This coupon entitles you to an energizing one-hour study break, followed by an hour of tutoring or helping you prepare for your next quiz or final.

**Dating Coupon**

SPLURGE

# Dating Coupon

This coupon is as good as money. It entitles you to $100 to spend together on a spontaneous date with the coupon giver. You must spend every penny!

**Dating Coupon**

SPLURGE

# Dating Coupon

This coupon entitles you to a pair of tickets to the concert of your choice. It also entitles you to a CD to listen to until the concert date arrives.

**Dating Coupon**

FUN AND FRUGAL

# Dating Coupon

This coupon entitles you to two movie tickets and a pound of your favorite candy, part of which we will share at the matinee of your choice.

**Dating Coupon**

SPLURGE

# Dating Coupon

This coupon entitles you to a romantic night out on the town, highlighted by a candlelight dinner and your choice of entertainment.

---

**Dating Coupon**

THOUGHTFUL

# Dating Coupon

This coupon is good for breakfast in bed. It includes a morning newspaper and permission to stay in bed as long as you desire.

---

**Dating Coupon**

SPORT AND LEISURE

# Dating Coupon

This coupon is good for a trip to the driving range to hit a bucket of golf balls, as well as some putting for kisses around the practice green.

---

**Dating Coupon**

SPORT AND LEISURE

# Dating Coupon

This coupon is good for a day trip to the mountains for your choice of hiking, skiing, fishing, or bird-watching.

# Dating Coupon

This coupon is good for a performing arts date—a play, opera, symphony, ballet, art-gallery show, or museum exhibit. Choose your favorite!

# Dating Coupon

This coupon entitles you to a theme date—you choose the theme. Example: "Foreign Theme"—Have dinner at a foreign restaurant, watch a foreign film, speak a foreign language, remove a foreign object, and so on!

# Dating Coupon

This coupon is good for a day of window-shopping, with a bonus: Within one week of the date, you will receive as a gift from me something that you admire, try on, or hint at during the date.

# Dating Coupon

This coupon is humbly presented by a coupon giver who would like to "get out of the doghouse." List your conditions here: _____

_____

**Dating Coupon**

OUTDOOR

# Dating Coupon

This coupon is good for a fun day in the big city. Museums, galleries, cafes—you name it!

---

**Dating Coupon**

OUTDOOR

# Dating Coupon

This coupon is good for a fun day in the country.
A picnic in a meadow, a bike ride around a lake—whatever you please!

---

**Dating Coupon**

SEASONAL

# Dating Coupon

This coupon entitles you to an Opening-Day Date—Baseball, plays, concert season, whatever you fancy.

---

**Dating Coupon**

SEASONAL

# Dating Coupon

This coupon invites you to a Winter Wonderland date that will include building a snowman together, taking a walk and having a snowball fight along the way, going on a sleigh ride, doing some sledding or skiing, and so on.

## Dating Coupon

**SPORT AND LEISURE**

# Dating Coupon

This coupon is good for a two-hour horseback ride, with a stop along the way for a secluded picnic.

## Dating Coupon

**THOUGHTFUL**

# Dating Coupon

This coupon entitles you to a relaxing champagne brunch on the weekend of your choice.

## Dating Coupon

**SPECIAL OCCASION**

# Dating Coupon

This coupon entitles you to a bonus birthday or anniversary celebration within one month from issue. The celebration will be accompanied by all the fanfare you would expect on your real birthday.

## Dating Coupon

**OUTDOOR**

# Dating Coupon

This coupon entitles you and me to $10 each in tickets for public transportation, which we will use together on the day of your choice. Let's see how far we can go!

**Dating Coupon**

RAINY DAY

# Dating Coupon

This coupon is good for an indoor "roast under the roof" (wieners and marshmallows) in my fireplace or wood stove.

---

**Dating Coupon**

WACKY AND WHIMSICAL

# Dating Coupon

This coupon entitles you to a date with me where we'll get wild and crazy with a paintbrush. We'll graffiti each other's plain white T-shirts using cloth paints, puff paint, felt markers, and so on, and then exchange them as gifts.

---

**Dating Coupon**

DOUBLE DATE

# Dating Coupon

This coupon is good for a double date with your parents or mine.

---

**Dating Coupon**

SEASONAL

# Dating Coupon

This coupon is good for a grand tour of your choice—a tour of homes, a garden tour, an art-gallery tour, or the Tour de France!

**Dating Coupon**

RELATIONSHIP BUILDING

# Dating Coupon

This coupon is good for a class we will take together, in the subject of your choice, such as sports, art, music, computers, cooking, dance, a foreign language, or landscaping.

---

**Dating Coupon**

SPECIAL OCCASION

# Dating Coupon

This valentine's coupon entitles you to ten thoughtful and romantic Valentine's Day gifts. The first five will be a love poem, a dozen roses, a box of candy, a romantic candlelight dinner, and lots of xoxo's. You get to choose the other five activities.

---

**Dating Coupon**

SEASONAL

# Dating Coupon

This coupon entitles you to a fun, romantic, and/or creative date that celebrates the season of your choice: winter, spring, summer, or fall.

---

**Dating Coupon**

OUT OF THE DOGHOUSE

# Dating Coupon

This "wild card" dating coupon entitles you to a Make Your Own Date—one that will prove to you how much I would like to get out of the doghouse. Planned or spontaneous, indoor or out, formal or informal—you choose.

**Dating Coupon**

SIMPLE AND FREE

# Dating Coupon

This coupon entitles you to have the most fun on a date that you've ever had for free. Money excluded. Lots of laughter included.

---

**Dating Coupon**

WACKY AND WHIMSICAL

# Dating Coupon

This coupon entitles you to a "Kidnapping" Date. Within the next ten days, you will be "kidnapped" by the coupon giver and whisked away for a clandestine time filled with surprise, mystery, and romance.

---

**Dating Coupon**

THOUGHTFUL

# Dating Coupon

This coupon entitles you to your favorite meal—cooked by me, of course—and the privilege of inviting the guest(s) of your choice to share it with us.

---

**Dating Coupon**

FUN AND FRUGAL

# Dating Coupon

This coupon is good for a date that appeals to all five senses: touch, sight, taste, smell, and sound.

**Dating Coupon**

ROMANTIC

# Dating Coupon

This coupon is good for the most mouthwatering dessert at the most romantic restaurant in town! Coffee or dessert wine included, too.

---

**Dating Coupon**

ROMANTIC

# Dating Coupon

This coupon entitles you to a picnic basket for two loaded with all of your favorite foods. You choose the setting.

---

**Dating Coupon**

RELATIONSHIP BUILDING

# Dating Coupon

This coupon is good for a Sentimental Flashback Date. Step back in time to recapture every moment of our very first date.

---

**Dating Coupon**

THOUGHTFUL

# Dating Coupon

This coupon entitles you to join the coupon giver in walking around town and performing random acts of kindness.

**Dating Coupon**

SPLURGE

# Dating Coupon

This coupon entitles you to join me on a date where we will be food connoisseurs/critics for the evening. Choose your favorite appetizer, and we'll enjoy it at three different restaurants, comparing the quality, taste, and price at each!

---

**Dating Coupon**

THOUGHTFUL

# Dating Coupon

This coupon is good for a 60-minute phone card or call from me the next time you leave town on business or vacation, so we can enjoy a long-distance telephone date.

---

**Dating Coupon**

FUN AND FRUGAL

# Dating Coupon

This coupon entitles you to the Fun and Frugal Date described below: _____

_____

_____

_____

---

**Dating Coupon**

ROMANTIC

# Dating Coupon

This coupon entitles you to the Romantic Date described below:_____

_____

_____

_____

**Dating Coupon**

**SPORT AND LEISURE**

# Dating Coupon

This coupon entitles you to the Sport and Leisure Date described below: _____
_____
_____
_____

---

**Dating Coupon**

**SIMPLE AND FREE**

# Dating Coupon

This coupon entitles you to the Simple and Free Date described below: _____
_____
_____
_____

---

**Dating Coupon**

**RAINY DAY**

# Dating Coupon

This coupon entitles you to the Rainy Day Date described below:_____
_____
_____
_____

---

**Dating Coupon**

**OUTDOOR**

# Dating Coupon

This coupon entitles you to the Outdoor Date described below:_____
_____
_____
_____

**Dating Coupon**

**DOUBLE DATE**

# Dating Coupon

This coupon entitles you to the Double Date described below:_____

_____

_____

_____

---

**Dating Coupon**

**SEASONAL/SPECIAL OCCASION**

# Dating Coupon

This coupon entitles you to the Seasonal or Special Occasion Date described below: _____

_____

_____

_____

---

**Dating Coupon**

**WACKY AND WHIMSICAL**

# Dating Coupon

This coupon entitles you to the Wacky and Whimsical Date described below: _____

_____

_____

_____

---

**Dating Coupon**

**SPLURGE**

# Dating Coupon

This coupon entitles you to the Splurge Date described below:_____

_____

_____

_____

**Dating Coupon**

# Dating Coupon

_____
_____
_____
_____
_____

**Dating Coupon**

# Dating Coupon

_____
_____
_____
_____
_____

**Dating Coupon**

# Dating Coupon

_____
_____
_____
_____
_____

**Dating Coupon**

# Dating Coupon

_____
_____
_____
_____
_____

# DATING INDEX

The dates in this book are organized according to categories. For a list of the icons and types of dates offered, see page xiv of the introduction. Of course, these categories are just suggestions. You can take any of these dates and adapt them to your own style and needs. Have fun!

 ## Anything Goes Date

## Friends First Date

## Great First Date

## Ideas to Spice Up Your Next Date

 **Last-Minute Date**

## Married Couples Date

 ## Out-of-the-Doghouse Date

**Relationship-Building Date**

## Sizzle Date

*Although the dates in this book are appropriate for any and all people, the following groupings are suggested date ideas for specific ages. As with the categories above, these are just suggestions.*

## Dates for Teenagers

# Dates for College Students

# Dates for Working People

## Proposal Dates

## Kid-Friendly Dates

# Dates for the Golden Years

# INDEX

# ABOUT THE AUTHOR

Steve Smith has been in the health and fitness industry for the past 14 years. In 1989, he managed the start-up of Toyota Motor Sales, U.S.A., Inc.'s corporate fitness center, where he remained fitness director for eight years. At Toyota, Smith developed a number of very successful programs, including the Swim to Catalina theme promotion, which received national recognition in USA Today's *USA Weekend* magazine. He also led Team Toyota to the National Corporate Sports Battle Championship, claiming the title of America's Most Fit Corporation in 1991 (nationally televised on ESPN TV).

From 1996 through 1998, Steve was regional director for the nation's largest corporate fitness management company, where he oversaw 20 corporate fitness centers, including Times Mirror Corporation, Los Angeles Times, Nissan, J. Paul Getty Trust, Sony Music, Hewlett Packard, Hitachi, Western Digital, and Mattel. In 1998, he co-founded Cornerstone Fitness, a corporate fitness consulting and management company based in the San Francisco/Bay Area.

Prior to entering into corporate fitness, Steve was president and owner of Body Design, a personal fitness training business based in Los Angeles. He provided fitness consulting and training services to several sports and television personalities. From 1993 through 1995, Steve played professional baseball for the Cleveland Indians in their minor league organization.

Smith earned his Bachelor of Science degree in physical education, with an emphasis in commercial and industrial fitness management, from Oregon State University. He enjoys playing golf, softball, jogging on the beach, camping, writing, and playing the piano. Steve was born in Dallas, Oregon, and currently resides in Scotts Valley, California.

# DO YOU HAVE A SPECIAL DATE STORY TO SHARE?

# WE WOULD LOVE TO HEAR IT.

Please send your story to:

Steve Smith
c/o Prima Publishing
P.O. Box 1260BK
Rocklin, CA 95677

Or submit your story to Prima's Web site at:
www.primalifestyles.com/cheapdates/

## Please Note

Prima may want to publish your story and your name in a future version of this book. By submitting a story, you agree that Prima shall own all rights to the story, including the right to publish the story and use your name in a future version of this book. Prima does not pay any compensation for the use of stories submitted. Stories should not be submitted by any person under the age of 18 and should not contain any obscene or graphic or explicit sexual material or any other illegal material of any kind.